THE OFFICIAL HISTORY (

POMPEY
CARDS & STICKERS

First published 2023

PHS Publishing
c/o Fratton Park
Frogmore Road
Portsmouth
PO4 8RA

www.pompeyhistory.org

Copyright © 2023 Ed Emptage.

The right of Ed Emptage to be identified as the author of this work has been asserted in accordance with the Copyright, Designs & Patents Act, 1988.

All rights reserved. No part of this book may be reprinted or reproduced or utilised in any form or by any electronic, mechanical or other means, now known or hereafter invented, including photocopying and recording, or in any information storage or retrieval system without permission in writing from the publishers. All images reproduced in this book are the copyright of their owners. Every effort has been made to contact the copyright holders of the images featured. Any enquiries concerning this please contact the publishers. Pompey History Society does not have any control over, or responsibility for, any third-party websites referred to in this book. All internet addresses given were correct at the time of going to print.

British Library Cataloguing in Publication Data. A catalogue record of this book is available from the British Library.

ISBN 978-1-7391813-2-1

Printed in Great Britain by Bishops Printers, Walton Road, Portsmouth PO6 1TR

Stickers and Albums courtesy of Panini S.p.A.

All Rights Reserved.

THE OFFICIAL HISTORY OF

POMPEY
CARDS & STICKERS

Ed Emptage

Foreword by Alan Knight MBE

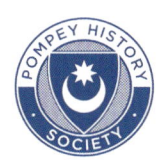

FOREWORD

When I was a kid growing up in Balham, like most of my football-mad friends, especially whenever there was a World Cup, one of the things we would always do is buy a sticker album from the local newsagents and start trying to fill it with the pictures of the stars of the day.

I particularly remember collecting coins given away at Esso petrol stations for the 1970 World Cup in Mexico – I'd have been about eight or nine then. That tournament wasn't one for the Goalkeepers' Union to remember as Peter Bonetti, for many, cost England a place in the semi-final, although I'd say he was let down by his defence!

Anyway, I digress. When I was offered the chance to write the foreword for The Official History of Pompey Cards & Stickers book, published to celebrate the club's 125th birthday, I was delighted to accept.

Anyone who, like me, remembers the thrill of buying a packet of cards and opening them to see the ones I didn't have already and then swapping the spares I obtained along the way with my mates, will be taken back in time by this book, especially when looking at the eras of their youth.

But, more than that, this book is an accessible window into the history of the club which has been a huge part of my life for the best part of 50 years now. It's been great to browse through it and see the players I played with and managers I played for, bringing back memories of some great games and characters.

What's more it's a comprehensive collection, lovingly detailing all the various publishers of cards and stickers down the years since the club's foundation in 1898. A complete set if you like. Which is better than I ever managed when collecting as kid...

Alan Knight MBE
801 appearances for Portsmouth FC (1978-2000)

BIBLIOGRAPHY

Pompey – The History of Portsmouth Football Club. Milestone Publications. 1984. Mike Neasom, Mick Cooper, Doug Robinson. **Half-Time (Football and the Cigarette Card, 1890–1940).** Murray Cards International. 1987. D. Thompson. **The Illustrated Footballer.** Breedon Books. 1989. Tony Ambrosen. **Toffee Cards: The Tobacco Years.** Skript Publishing. 1997. David France. **Portsmouth Football Club – The Official Pictorial History.** Bishops Printers. 1998. Peter Jeffs, Colin Farmery, Richard Owen. **Pompey People – Portsmouth F.C. Who's Who 1899–2000.** Yore Publications. 2000. Mick Cooper. **Pompey Players 1920–2001.** Bishops Printers. 2001. Roger Holmes. **Swap Yer! The Wonderful World of Football Cards and Sticker Albums.** Orion. 2005. Rob Jovanovic. **Toffee Cards – The Bubblegum Years.** Skript Publishing. 2006. David France, Barry Hewitt. **Huddersfield Town Cards and Stickers.** 2008. Roger Pashby. **The Red Men of Liverpool Football Club.** deCoubertin Books. 2017. G.A. Rowlands. **An A-to-Z of Football Collectibles: Priceless Cigarette Cards and Sought-after Soccer Stickers.** Pitch Publishing. 2019. Carl Wilkes.

WEBSITES

cardhawkuk.com
cards.littleoak.com.au/index.html
cartophilic-info-exch.blogspot.co.uk
chrisdlee.com
facebook.com/groups/vintagefootballcards
footballsoccercards.com
footballstickipedia.com
huddersfieldtowncollection.wordpress.com
pinnacecards.wordpress.com
pompeyrama.com
taddyprominentfootballers.wordpress.com
theyflysohigh.co.uk

IMAGE CREDITS

Garry Daynes: Crescent Confectionery. J.A. Mackie *(page 49)*, Teasdale & Co. F. Worrall *(page 54)*.
Nigel Eastman: St Petersburg Cigarette Co. Ltd. D. Cunliffe, H. Stringfellow *(page 16)*.
Ben Hardinge: Topps/Portsmouth FC. 2008 FA Cup Winners Limited Edition Collectors Box Set cards *(page 191)*.
Paul Jeggo: Match!. Lomana LuaLua *(page 175)*, Jermain Defoe *(page 180)*.
Lockdales Auctioneers and Valuers: W.D. & H.O. Wills. The Life of H.M. King Edward VIII, At The Cup Final, 1929 *(page 69)*.
Roger Pashby: Pinnace small-size. J. Armstrong *(page 28)*, R. Davies, A. Meikle *(page 29)*.
Michael Prior: St Petersburg Cigarette Co. Ltd. T. Wilkie *(page 16)*.
Matt Stevens: Taddy & Co. Prominent Footballers, London Mixture cards *(page 23)*, Pinnace team, Portsmouth A.F.C. *(page 31)*.
Carl Wilkes: The Wizard. Footballers and Secret Signs shield and envelope, F. Cook *(page 45)*.

DEDICATION

I would like to dedicate this book to my wife Alison ("how's the book going?"), children Emily and Daniel, mum and dad and brother James, and to all the members of my Pompey family I have met along the way.

Player appearances and goals figures include those made as a substitute and every effort has been made to ensure their accuracy.

CONTENTS

PORTSMOUTH FC – A BRIEF HISTORY		8
INTRODUCTION		11
THE SOUTHERN LEAGUE	1900–1919	14
THE FOOTBALL LEAGUE	1920–1929	26
THIRD TIME LUCKY	1930–1939	46
BACK-TO-BACK CHAMPIONS	1940–1959	78
SECOND DIVISION CONSOLIDATION	1960–1969	114
FREEFALL	1970–1979	126
THE CLIMB BACK TO THE FIRST DIVISION	1980–1989	136
FA CUP AND PROMOTION HEARTBREAK	1990–1999	148
THE PREMIER LEAGUE AND FA CUP GLORY	2000–2010	162
THE PST AND THE TORNANTE COMPANY	2011–2022	182
COMPLETE CARDS AND STICKERS LISTS		196

PORTSMOUTH FC – A BRIEF HISTORY

The city of Portsmouth has had a strong football tradition right from the days of Sherlock Holmes author Arthur Conan Doyle playing football in the city in the late 1880s, through to the exploits of the Royal Artillery team, based at Burnaby Road, which was among the foremost amateur sides in the country in the late 1890s.

This enthusiasm helped lead to the formation of Pompey – as the club is known around the globe – in April 1898. Success came quickly, with the Southern League won in 1902 and again in 1920, when the club joined The Football League.

By 1927 the club had been promoted twice and found itself in the First Division. Pompey quickly established themselves as the prominent club south of London, three times reaching the FA Cup Final in 1929, 1934 and 1939. The latter visit saw the team defy the odds, beating Wolverhampton Wanderers 4-1 to take the cup south of London for the first time. However it was after the war that the team came into its own, with a formidable scouting operation creating the 'team with no stars' which would win consecutive league titles in 1949 and 1950. Few clubs have repeated the feat since.

Since those halcyon days, being a Pompey fan has never been dull, rollercoasting through the divisions almost at will. By 1978 the club had fallen to the Fourth Division, but revived to return to the First Division just nine years later.

In 2003 the club would be back in the limelight, winning promotion to the Premier League.

Bankrolled by Sacha Gaydamak, glory returned in 2008 when Pompey were cup winners again and AC Milan came to town as Fratton Park hosted elite European football for the first time.

Financial catastrophe followed and by 2013 the club was back in the fourth tier, now owned by the fans. Under community ownership the League Two title was won in 2017 and the green shoots of revival have sprouted again.

Portsmouth FC has a long and rich heritage and the Pompey History Society was founded by a group of supporters as a non-profit organisation who were keen to ensure the club's archive is preserved for future generations.

Supporting publication projects is another arm of the society's social work, so it is delighted to have played its part in bringing this comprehensive book of Pompey cards and stickers to fruition.

For more information on the society and its activities visit **www.pompeyhistory.org** or email **history@pompeyfc.co.uk**

OLDHAM R.F.C.

PARTICK TH...

...M FOREST

89 P. GUNTER RIGHT BACK

90 B. JACKSON

WING HALF

PORTSMOUTH

...ADOWN

PORT V...

94 ...QUHART OUTSIDE L...

95 ...NIVEN

CENTRE...

INTRODUCTION

Footballers have featured on collectible cards and stickers since the 1880s. The earliest cards were sold in packets by firms such as J. Baines and collected by schoolboys in huge numbers. In the United States during the late 1800s, adverts were printed on to cardboard 'stiffeners' and inserted into packets of cigarettes to protect the contents from being crushed. Before long, tobacco firms replaced these advertisement cards with collectible thematic sets to encourage customer loyalty to their brands of cigarettes, establishing a marketing gimmick which soon made its way across the Atlantic.

At a time when a large proportion of the adult population smoked, the tobacco industry boomed and competition between rival firms was fierce. As each clamoured to increase their share of the market, huge effort was put into producing the most desirable cards. Football was fast becoming a national obsession in the UK and in the days before newspapers were printed in colour, and long before the introduction of colour television, there was great demand for images of the players and teams that supporters watched from the terraces. As printing techniques developed, the early black and white cards were replaced by colourful sets of players complete with detailed biographies on the reverse.

Although marketed to adult smokers, football cigarette cards often found their way into the hands of children who would collect their favourite clubs and players. During the 1920s, publishers of boys' papers picked up on this trend and began issuing cards with their publications. At the same time, manufacturers of products as diverse as confectionery and gravy salt also gave away cards with their goods. The popularity of cigarette cards reached its peak during the 1930s and by the time World War Two broke out, thousands of sets depicting hundreds of subjects had been issued.

However, a combination of rationing and the lack of raw materials for paper production meant cigarette cards were issued in ever-dwindling numbers immediately after the war. The gap in the market was soon filled by confectionery firms such as Barratt & Co., who had first produced football cards during the 1920s. Their Famous Footballers sets were issued each season with packets of sweet cigarettes over several decades.

In the 1950s, various firms issued cards with an accompanying piece of bubble gum, either from a vending machine or wrapped up together in a packet, continuing a trend which started in the 1920s. Chix Confectionery and Master Vending released a limited number of sets, but A&BC's colourful football cards proved extremely popular and were produced until the mid-1970s. Cards remained the main focus of the football collectibles market until the late 1960s when FKS introduced the 'picture stamp' album to the UK. A forerunner to the self-adhesive sticker album, the earliest FKS collections featured pictures which had to be glued into position, and it wasn't until the 1970s that stickers with peelable backs became commonplace. Italian firm Panini introduced their first British domestic football sticker album in 1978 and cornered the market until 1994 when Merlin Publishing acquired the license to publish the only Premier League sticker album in the UK. During the past two decades, Panini and Topps have come to dominate the global football card and sticker industry.

In compiling this book I have included cards and stickers from as many different sets and albums as possible. While researching my own collection it soon became apparent that it would be an impossible task to try and catalogue every Portsmouth item ever issued, let alone source copies of them all. In fact, several of those featured only came to light in the months and weeks before publication. The majority can be purchased through specialist online dealers and auction sites for very little outlay. Others are extremely scarce and in some cases would command high prices, if you are able to find them. Collectively they provided a unique photographic and illustrative record of those who have entertained generations of Portsmouth

Football Club's supporters for the past 125 years. From the earliest black and white cigarette cards issued at the turn of the twentieth century, through to modern trading cards embedded with sections of match-worn shirts, Pompey's players and teams have been documented on these collectible curiosities for almost as long as the club has been in existence. Some of those featured are among the most famous in the club's history, others a mere footnote. Some you may have seen play, others your parents or grandparents may have told you about. You may have collected some of the cards and stickers in the past, or started putting a collection together recently. I hope that the images within these pages rekindle memories of both supporting Pompey through the years and the simple pleasure of collecting, and that this book serves as a useful resource to both new and seasoned collectors alike.

ACKNOWLEDGEMENTS

Although the majority of the cards and stickers are from my own collection, I would like to thank Garry Daynes, Nigel Eastman, Ben Hardinge, Paul Jeggo, Roger Pashby, Michael Prior, Matt Stevens, Carl Wilkes, the Cartophilic Society of Great Britain and Lockdales Auctioneers & Valuers for supplying additional images. I am indebted to the late Bill Priddy, whose generosity with both his time and access to his collection played a huge part in getting this project off the ground.

Details surrounding the cards and stickers have been gleaned from several sources, in particular Alan Jenkins' Football Cartophilic Info Exchange blog – cartophilic-info-exch.blogspot.com – which has been an invaluable resource. Finally, thank you to the Pompey History Society, Portsmouth Football Club and Bishops Printers for supporting this publication, and to Paul Boynton, Mick Comben and Colin Farmery for their help with proofreading and fact-checking the content.

THE SOUTHERN LEAGUE

The popularity and success of local amateur side Royal Artillery had fuelled the desire for a professional club in Portsmouth and following a meeting of local sportsmen and businessmen on 5th April 1898, Portsmouth Football and Athletic Company was formed. Farmland close to Fratton railway station was purchased, a pitch laid, stands erected on the north and south sides, and the club successfully applied for admission to the Southern League First Division in time for the 1899/1900 season. An impressive 20 wins from 28 games under the guidance of manager Frank Brettell secured a second-place finish behind champions Tottenham Hotspur and just two years later Pompey went one better, winning the title for the first time in 1902.

Pompey finished no lower than ninth-place between 1899 and 1910 before their form hit a disastrous slump in 1910/11. Just eight wins from 38 matches resulted in a bottom-place finish and relegation to the Second Division. Pompey succeeded in gaining promotion after just one season in the second tier but a year out of the top-flight had compounded debt that had been increasing at an alarming rate for several years. The winding up of the original company and the formation of the new Portsmouth Football Company, backed by guarantees to the bank from the directors, brought some much-needed stability before the outbreak of World War One and suspension of competitive football in 1915.

When football resumed in 1919/20, Pompey won the Southern League championship for a second time. The club were ambitious and the prestige and riches of The Football League proved too attractive to ignore. Pompey were elected to join the newly-formed Third Division South ahead of the 1920/21 season, ready to compete at a national level for the first time.

1900–1919

ST. PETERSBURG CIGARETTE CO. LTD. 1900.

Footballers

17 known cards. Unnumbered.
D. Cunliffe, T. Wilkie, H. Stringfellow.
(68 x 40mm).

The first cigarette cards to feature Portsmouth players were issued in 1900 by local firm St. Petersburg Cigarette Co. Ltd., of High Street, Old Portsmouth. These cards are exceptionally scarce, with only 17 known varieties in existence.

The series included Dan Cunliffe, Thomas Wilkie and Harold Stringfellow who all signed for Pompey in 1899 and appeared in the club's first competitive fixture, a 1-0 victory away to Chatham on 2nd September the same year.

Ex-Liverpool inside-forward Dan Cunliffe signed from New Brighton Tower. He returned to his former club the following year before re-joining Pompey in 1901. Cunliffe spent a further five seasons at Fratton Park before leaving for New Brompton in 1906 having made 255 league appearances, scoring 144 goals.

Left-back Thomas Wilkie began his career in Scotland with Heart of Midlothian before joining Pompey from Liverpool, making 178 appearances during four seasons with the club.

Harold Stringfellow signed from Everton and went on to make 218 appearances. The centre-half was made vice captain for the 1903/04 season.

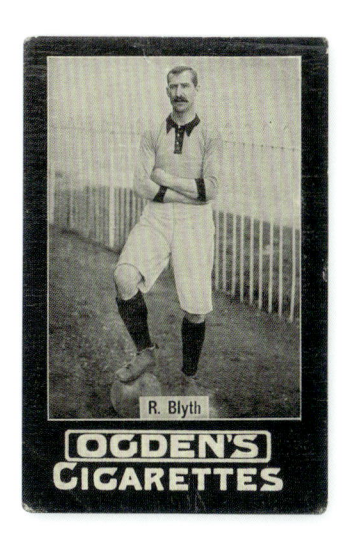

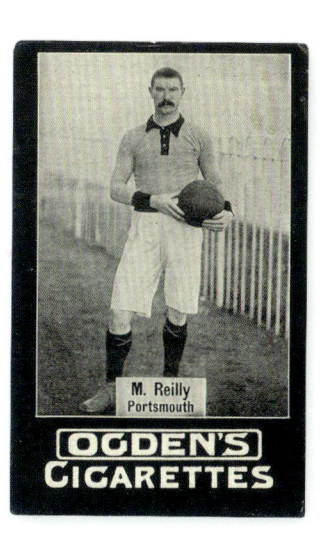

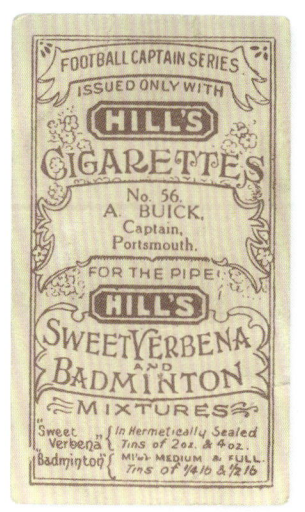

OGDEN'S. 1902.
General Interest

300 cards. Unnumbered. R. Blyth, M. Reilly, S. Smith. (62 x 40mm).

Bob Blyth and Matt Reilly were two of the three Pompey players included in the Ogden's *General Interest* series.

Bob Blyth, Pompey's first captain, joined in 1899 and served as player-manager between 1901 and 1904, making a total of 154 appearances. He was elected to the board of directors in 1909, before becoming vice-chairman in 1920 and then chairman in 1924.

Ireland international goalkeeper Matt Reilly, Pompey's first-ever signing, was well-known locally having previously played for Royal Artillery. He made 227 appearances between 1899 and 1904 before signing for Dundee.

R. & J. HILL. 1906.
Football Captain Series

20 cards (Nos. 41–60).
No. 56. A. Buick. (65 x 37mm).

TADDY & CO. 1907.

Prominent Footballers (1st Series)

595 cards. Unnumbered. Two back designs: Grapnel Mixture (g), Imperial Tobacco (i). M.W. Allman (i), J. Bellamy (g), T. Birtles (g), T. Bowman (g), A. Buick (i), F. Clipstone (g), W. Cooper (g), H. Digweed (i), W. Kirby (i), E. McDonald (g), G. Philip (i), W. Smith (i), H. Thompson (g), R. Walker (g), D. Wilson (i). (67 x 36mm).

Taddy & Co. issued approximately 1,400 *Prominent Footballers* cards across three series in 1907, 1908 and 1913/14.

The first series featured 15 Portsmouth players including centre-forward William 'Sunny Jim' Kirby who signed from Swindon Town in September 1905. He scored 78 goals in 224 Southern League matches before moving to Preston North End in 1911.

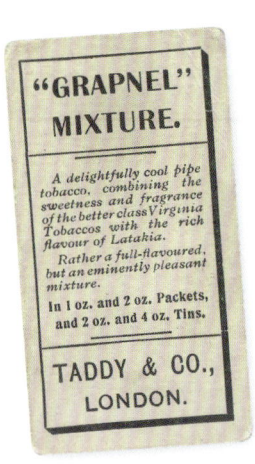

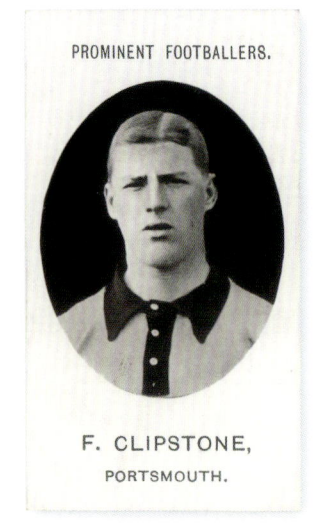

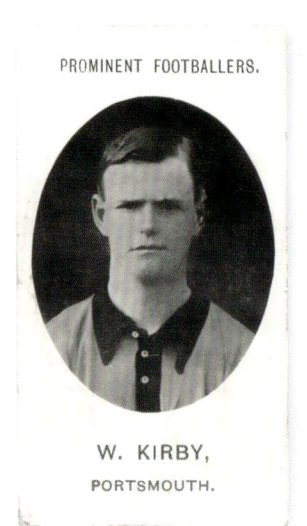

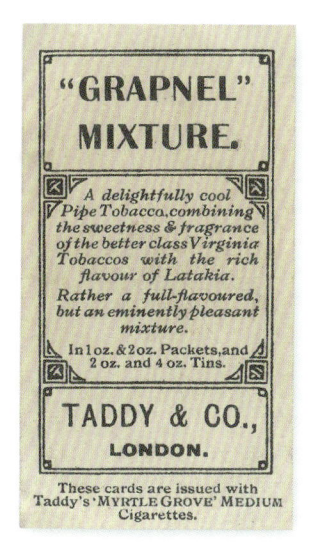

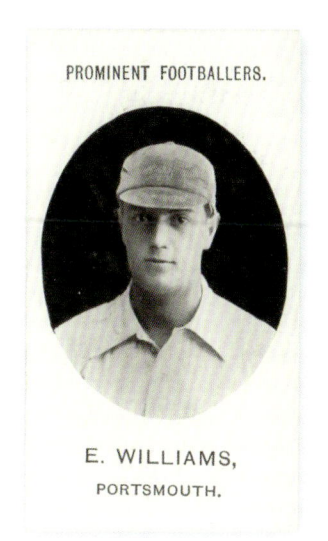

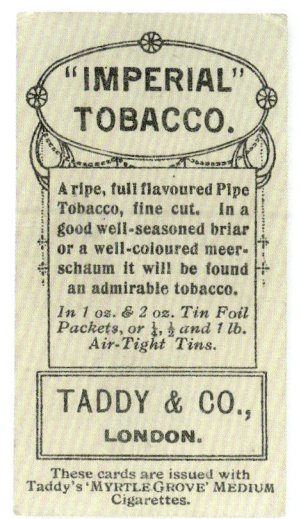

TADDY & CO. 1908/09.

Prominent Footballers (2nd Series)

400 cards. Unnumbered. Two back designs: Grapnel Mixture (g), Imperial Tobacco (i). Cameron (i), G.W. Churchill (g), W. Gisborne (g), L.A. Louch (g), E. Williams (i), W. Yates (i). (67 x 36mm).

Six Pompey players, including left-half George Churchill and Ryde-born left-winger Ernest Williams, featured in the second *Prominent Footballers* series.

Churchill's Pompey career was short-lived with only three Western League matches and one friendly to his name.

Williams represented England as an amateur and is pictured wearing one of his international caps. He had two spells with Pompey, the first between 1906 and 1909, before returning for the 1910/11 season following a year with Chelsea. Williams made a total of 36 appearances, scoring seven goals.

W.D. & H.O. WILLS. 1907.
Football Club Colours

50 cards. Unnumbered. Portsmouth. (64 x 36mm).

Pompey's first strip of a salmon pink shirt with maroon collar and cuffs and white shorts earned the club the nickname 'The Shrimps'.

Wills' Scissors cigarettes were issued to servicemen stationed in India and advertised as being 'Special Army Quality'.

COHEN WEENEN & CO. 1907/08.
Football Captains 1907–8

60 cards. Unnumbered. A. Buick. (63 x 35mm).

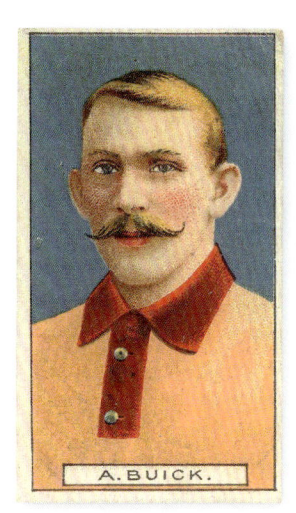

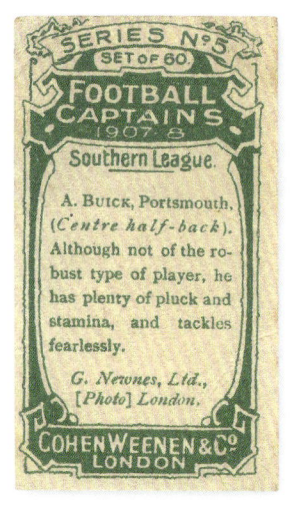

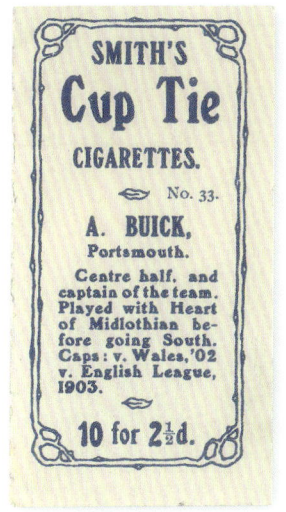

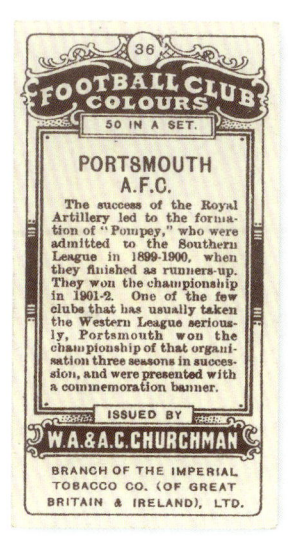

F. & J. SMITH. 1908.

Footballers

100 cards. No. 33. Albert Buick. (67 x 35mm).

Scottish centre-half and Pompey captain Albert Buick joined from Heart of Midlothian in 1903. He played almost 300 games before leaving the club during the 1910/11 season. Buick earned two international caps versus Ireland and Wales in 1902, scoring on both occasions.

W.A. & A.C CHURCHMAN. 1909.

Football Club Colours

50 cards. No. 36. Portsmouth A.F.C. (67 x 35mm).

Identical series with different backs were issued by Ogden's in 1906 and Franklyn Davey & Co. in 1909.

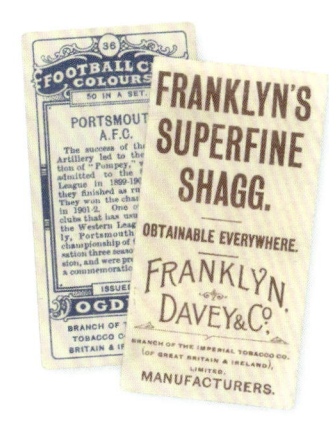

GALLAHER. 1910.

Association Football Club Colours

100 cards. No. 43. J. Warner. (63 x 38mm).

The 1909/10 season saw Pompey switch from salmon pink to white shirts, as illustrated in Gallaher's *Association Football Club Colours* series. Full-back Jack Warner made 227 Southern League appearances between 1906 and 1915. When a knee injury brought his playing career to an end he was employed as trainer, a position he held for almost 20 years. The cards in this series can be found with both grey and brown borders.

OGDEN'S. 1910.

Club Colour Badges

43 cards. Unnumbered. Portsmouth. (63 x 32mm).

W.D. & H.O. WILLS. 1914.

Famous Footballers

50 cards. No. 2. A.E. Knight. (64 x 35mm).

Arthur Knight made 157 Southern League and 34 Football League appearances between 1909 and 1922. An England amateur international full-back, he played 30 games for his country and in all three matches for Great Britain's gold medal-winning team at the 1912 Summer Olympics in Stockholm. Knight also gained one full England cap, captaining the side versus Ireland in 1919. The reverse can be found with two different designs.

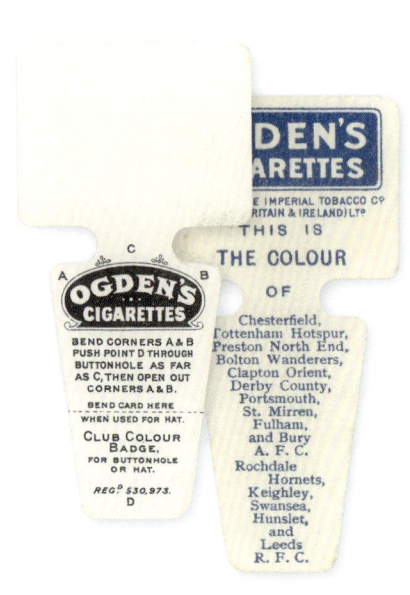

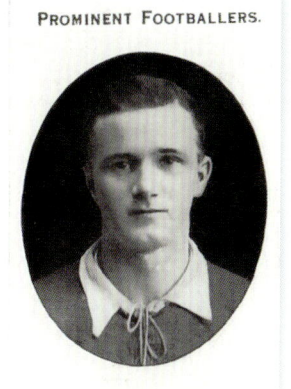

TADDY & CO. 1913/14.

Prominent Footballers (3rd series)

408 known cards. Unnumbered. London Mixture backs. J. Armstrong, G. Arnold, H. Buddery, J. Harwood, J. Hogg, W.E. James, A. Knight, J. Probert, F. Stringfellow, E. Thompson, J. Turner, S. Upton, J. Walls, J. Warner. (69 x 36mm).

Taddy & Co. released their third and final series of *Prominent Footballers* during the 1913/14 season. James 'Joe' Armstrong, Harold Buddery and William 'Billy' James were all forwards who represented Pompey in the Southern League, and each found the net during the club's first season in the Football League in 1920/21. James scored Pompey's first Football League goal in a 3-0 victory at home to Swansea Town.

W.A. & A.C. CHURCHMAN. 1914/15.
Footballers

50 cards. No. 48. A.E. Knight.
(36 x 68mm).

W.A. & A.C. Churchman's set of 50 *Footballers* featured Pompey's royal blue shirt, adopted in 1912/13, on a card in colour for the first time.

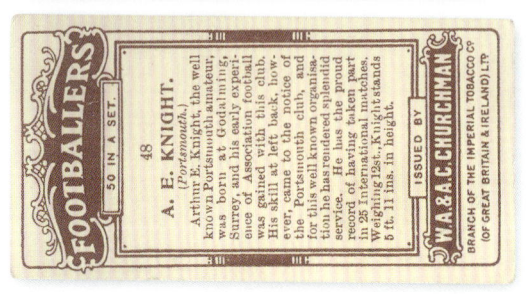

F. & J. SMITH. 1917.
Football Club Records (1916/17)

50 cards. No. 40. Portsmouth. A.E. Knight. O.H.M.S. (67 x 35mm).

Cigarette card production ground almost to a complete halt in 1915 as resources were conserved for the war effort. One of very few series issued during this period, however, was F. & J. Smith's *Football Club Records* in 1917. Arthur Knight's service in the Army is referenced with O.H.M.S. (On His Majesty's Service) on the front of the card. The reverse lists the club's London Combination Wartime League 1916/17 results.

J. BAINES. 1910–1918.

Gold Medal Football Cards

Unknown number in series. Unnumbered. Portsmouth. (80 x 68mm).

J. Baines Ltd. of Bradford was one of the earliest producers of football cards which pre-dated the cigarette variety by several years. Proprietor John Baines, the self-proclaimed 'Football Card King', was an eccentric figure whose shield-shaped *Gold Medal Football Cards* were keenly collected by schoolboys. Baines also issued cards covering a wide range of sports including rugby, cricket and golf.

These are often found in poor condition which can in some cases be attributed to games including 'who's nearest?' and 'skagging', during which players would take turns to flick cards against a wall. The rules of the games varied, but it is thought that the player whose card landed closest to the wall, or landed on top of another, collected all of the cards.

THE FOOTBALL LEAGUE

Pompey were promoted to the Second Division as champions in May 1924, losing only seven of their 42 fixtures on the way to claiming the title. An impressive fourth-place finish during the first season in the second tier was followed by a mid-table finish a year later. In 1926/27, promotion was achieved yet again. Pompey finished in second place behind Middlesbrough, pipping Manchester City to promotion on the last day of the season by the narrowest of margins with a goal average of 1.77551 to City's 1.77049. Pompey had reached the First Division just seven years after making their Football League debut, and were the first club south of London to achieve the feat.

At the end of the season manager John McCartney, who had overseen the club's rise through the divisions, stepped down due to ill-health and was replaced by Jack Tinn. Pompey struggled with the demands of top-flight football during the first two seasons of Tinn's leadership and fought a constant battle against relegation. A series of heavy defeats included the record 10-0 reverse away to Leicester City.

In stark contrast to Pompey's dismal league form, an impressive run in the FA Cup saw them progress to the final for the first time in 1929. A crowd of over 39,000 witnessed the 3-2 quarter-final victory over West Ham United at Fratton Park before a 1-0 defeat of Aston Villa at Highbury set up a meeting with Bolton Wanderers at Wembley. Pompey began the game positively and had the better of the first half exchanges. However, a torn muscle sustained by left-back Tommy Bell just before half-time disrupted the side's rhythm as he was forced play the second half heavily bandaged and limping on the wing. Two goals in the final 11 minutes sealed a 2-0 victory for Wanderers as Pompey's players and supporters were made to wait for their first taste of FA Cup silverware.

1920–1929

GODFREY PHILLIPS.
PINNACE CIGARETTES. 1920-23.

Footballers (small-size)

2462 cards. No. 169. W. Probert, No. 170. F. Stringfellow, No. 171. A.E. Knight, No. 172. J. Armstrong, No. 424. J.A. Hogg, No. 425. J. Harwood, No. 534. E.R. Robson, No. 535. H. Buddery, No. 536. J. Turner.

Between 1920 and 1923, Godfrey Phillips released a huge photographic collection of 2,462 football and rugby league player portraits with their Pinnace brand of cigarettes. The earliest sets featured four players per club, with later releases including the starting eleven. One card was given away with packets of ten cigarettes, two with packets of twenty. Variations can be found in the design on the reverse of the cards, the size of the picture, the colour of the background and the position of the number.

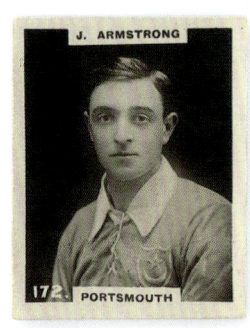

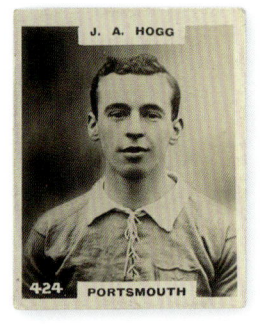

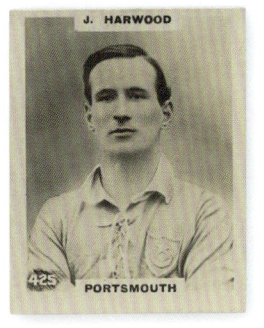

28 | THE OFFICIAL HISTORY OF POMPEY CARDS & STICKERS

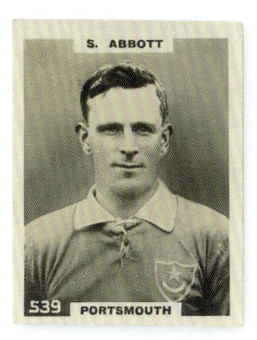

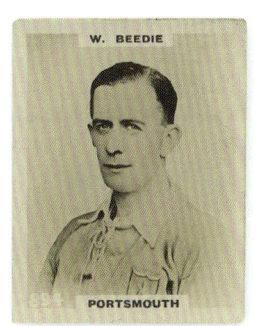

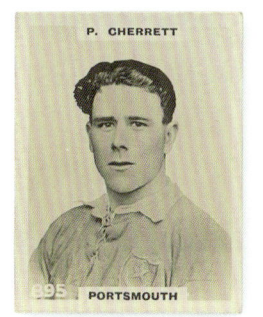

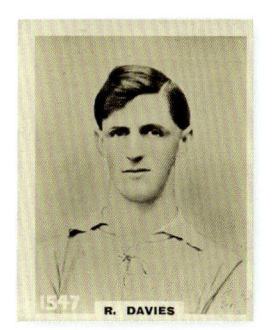

Continued

No. 539. S. Abbott, No. 776. Z. March, No. 894. W. Beedie, No. 895. P. Cherrett, No. 896. J. Martin, No. 1547. R. Davies, No. 1548. E. Gadsden, No. 1549. G. McGee, No. 1550. A. Meikle.

1920–1929 | 29

Continued

No. 1551. H. Abbott, No. 1552. J. Kennedy, No. 1553. J.R. Wilson, No. 1554. J. Mackie, No. 1555. R.V. Hoten. (45 x 35mm).

FOOTBALL & SPORTS FAVOURITE AND SPORTS FUN. 1922.

Sportsmen

168 paper stamps. Unnumbered. A.E. Knight. (40 x 40mm).

Issued as sheets of adhesive-backed stamps which could be cut out and stuck into an accompanying album.

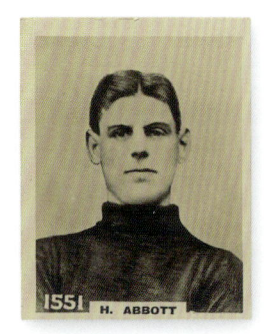

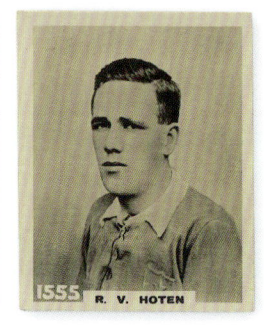

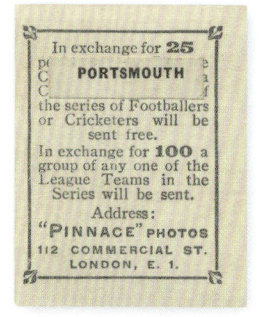

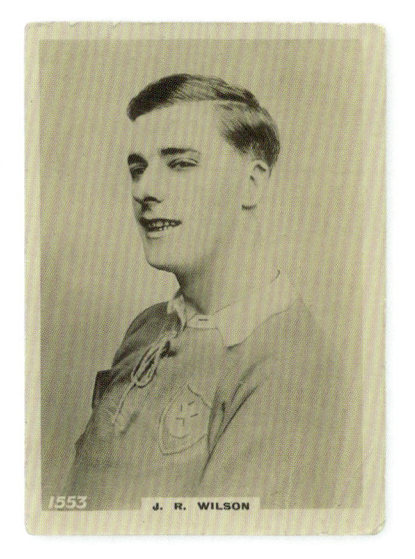

GODFREY PHILLIPS. PINNACE CIGARETTES. 1920–23.

Footballers (large-size)

Unknown number in series.
No. 1553. J.R. Wilson. (82 x 58mm).

Large-size cards were issued with boxes of 50 and 100 cigarettes. Half-back John Wilson joined Pompey in February 1921 and made 63 league and cup appearances before switching to Reading in 1923.

Team cards (cabinet-size)

86 known cards. Unnumbered. Portsmouth A.F.C. 1920–1921. (128 x 180mm).

Cabinet-size team cards could be sent away for in exchange for 100 small-size, or 20 large-size cards. This card shows the Portsmouth squad with the Southern League championship shield won in 1919/20. Pinnace team cards are extremely scarce and sell for large sums when they come up for sale.

GODFREY PHILLIPS.
PINNACE CIGARETTES. 1920–23.

Footballers (cabinet-size)

Unknown number in series.
No. 424. J.A. Hogg. (150 x 100mm).

Cabinet-size player cards were available in exchange for 25 small-size cards or five large-size cards.

Outside-right James Hogg joined Pompey from South Shields in 1913. He featured for the club during World War One, and was an important figure in the club's Southern League title-winning side of 1919/20. Hogg made 16 appearances during Pompey's debut season in the Football League, scoring two goals, before signing for Guildford City.

GODFREY PHILLIPS.
B.D.V. CIGARETTES. 1920.

League Colours

90 known 'silks'. Unnumbered. Portsmouth. Large (150 x 100mm), small (68 x 49mm).

Rectangles of silk-like material, both printed and embroidered, were issued with tobacco products for several years. These were especially popular with female smokers as they could be stitched together to create quilts and pillowcases. Godfrey Phillips' *League Colours* series was produced in two sizes and was one of the last of its kind to be issued by the company.

SPORT AND ADVENTURE. 1922.

Famous Footballers

46 cards. No. 32. A.E. Knight. (70 x 42mm).

Sport and Adventure's series of 46 *Famous Footballers* was issued in pairs, or strips of three cards.

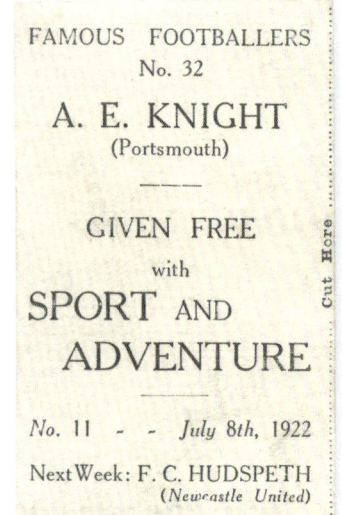

F. & J. SMITH. 1922.

Football Club Records (1921/22)

50 cards. No. 40. Portsmouth. A.E. Knight. (67 x 35mm).

The 1922 update to the 1917 *Football Club Records* series again featured Arthur Knight. Pompey's results from the 1921/22 season are listed on the reverse.

ADVENTURE. 1923.

Famous Club Colours and Players

12 sheets of nine players. Unnumbered. S.W. Abbott (spelt incorrectly on card), Portsmouth. (62 x 42mm).

Shirley Abbott joined Pompey from Derby County in 1913 and played at left-half and centre-half in the Southern League. He went on to make 100 Football League and FA Cup appearances, primarily at left-back, between 1921 and 1923 before transferring to Queens Park Rangers. This paper cut-out was taken from the first in a series of twelve sheets issued with Adventure in 1923.

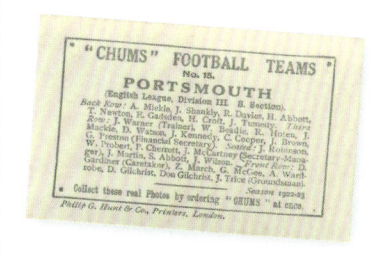

CHUMS. 1922.

"Chums" Football Teams

20 cards. No. 15. Portsmouth.
(43 x 70mm).

BUCKTROUT & CO. 1924.

Football Clubs

50 cards. No. 46. Portsmouth.
(47 x 68mm).

Distributed in the Channel Islands by Guernsey-based tobacco firm Bucktrout and Co. Ltd. All the cards in this series feature squad photographs except the Portsmouth card which is a composite image of individual portraits.

COMPTONS GRAVY SALT. 1924/25.

Football Clubs (Series B, Division 2)

22 cards. No. 16. Portsmouth. (64 x 35mm).

Comptons of Sheffield issued several series of both black and white and colour *Football Clubs* cards with tins of gravy salt between 1924 and 1927. Cards from these series are often found creased due to the way that they were packed into the tins.

LACEY'S CHEWING WAX. 1925.

Footballers

50 cards. No. 33. J. Mackie. (68 x 35mm).

Lacey's series of *Footballers* featured inside-forward James 'Jerry' Mackie. He joined Pompey from Blantyre Celtic in 1920 and went on to form a fruitful attacking partnership with Billy Haines. The reverse of the cards in this series can be found with two different designs.

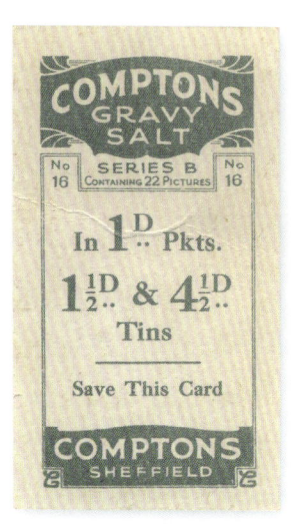

S. BINKS, PORTSMOUTH

R. DAVIES, PORTSMOUTH

J. MACKIE, PORTSMOUTH

J. MARTIN, PORTSMOUTH

BUY BARRATT & CO.'S SHERBET NOVELTIES.

BARRATT'S XMAS CLUB BOXES ARE THE BEST. ORDER YOURS EARLY

BARRATT & CO. 1925–28.

Cricketers, Footballers and Football Teams

200+ cards. Unnumbered.
S. Binks, R. Davies, J. Mackie,
J. Martin, A. Meikle. (63 x 35mm).

Confectionery firm Barratt & Co. began inserting football cards into packets of sweet cigarettes during the 1920s and became a prolific distributor of collectible cards for several decades.

The *Cricketers, Footballers and Football Teams* series featured five Pompey players including Sydney Binks, who joined from Blackpool in 1927. Binks had previously played for Huddersfield Town and is pictured wearing a Town shirt. He played for Pompey reserves several times but left the club the following year without a first-team appearance to his name.

V.C.C. 1922/23.
Sportsmen and Other Notabilities

72 cards. No. 19. E.R. Robson. (60 x 38mm).

Goalkeeper Edward 'Ned' Robson's three-year Pompey career ended abruptly in 1922 when he dislocated a finger during a match at Southampton. He transferred to Sunderland then went on to play for Swansea Town, Wrexham and Rochdale.

GALLAHER. 1926.
Famous Footballers

50 cards. No. 40. James Martin. (64 x 38mm).

Left-half James Martin served Pompey for seven years as the club rose through the divisions. When he was released by manager Jack Tinn in 1927, Martin joined Aldershot having scored 29 goals in 226 appearances.

CRESCENT CONFECTIONERY. 1925.
Footballers

100 cards. Unnumbered. R. Davies. (54 x 37mm).

Crescent Confectionery's scarce series of *Footballers* featured wing-half Reginald Davies who signed from non-league Sutton United in 1922. He made 216 appearances before signing for Brentford in the summer of 1927.

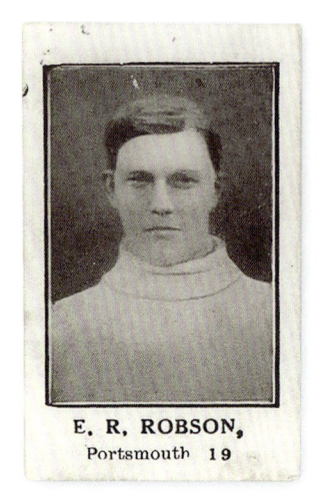

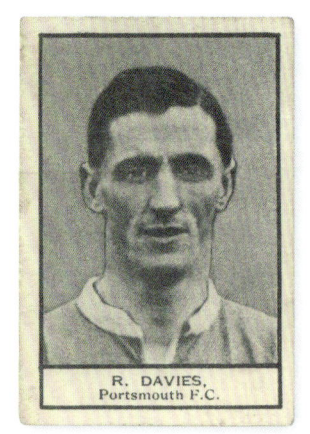

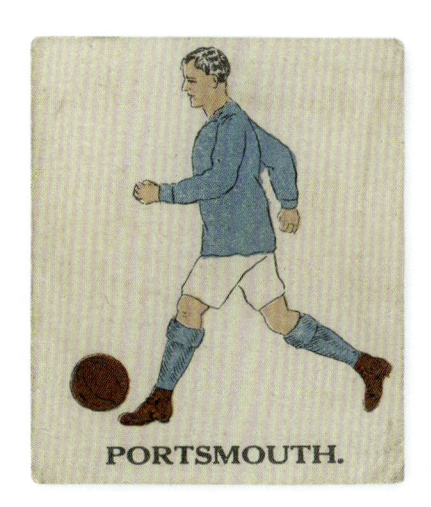

J.C. BATTOCK. 1923/24.
Football & Cricket Cards

108 cards. Unnumbered. Portsmouth. (70 x 58mm).

J.C. Battock produced several series of football cards during the 1920s. The reverse of the cards suggested they could be used to play games such as 'snap' and 'skimmer cards' as well as being collected and redeemed in exchange for a gift. Issued during the 1923/24 season, this particular series covered 108 football clubs of the English First, Second and Third (North and South) divisions, plus the 20 of the Scottish First Division. Variations in the illustration, typeface and punctuation can be found on the front of the cards and there are eight different back designs.

J.C. BATTOCK. 1924/25.
Football & Cricket Cards

21 known cards. Unnumbered. Portsmouth. (70 x 58mm).

The following season J.C. Battock issued a series of black and white cards which could be coloured in and sent away for the chance to win a prize.

PALS. 1923.

"Pals" New Football Series

30 cards. Unnumbered. Portsmouth F.C. (73 x 91mm).

Originally issued as a pair with Sunderland F.C.

JOHN PLAYER & SONS. 1927.

Football Caricatures by 'Mac'

50 cards. No. 13. Harry Foxall. (67 x 35mm).

Harry Foxall was ever-present in central defence as Pompey achieved promotion to the First Division in 1927. The following season he lost his place in the side to John McIlwaine and joined Kidderminster Harriers having made 166 league and cup appearances. This series was illustrated by George Douglas Machin, a sports cartoonist at the Daily Mirror.

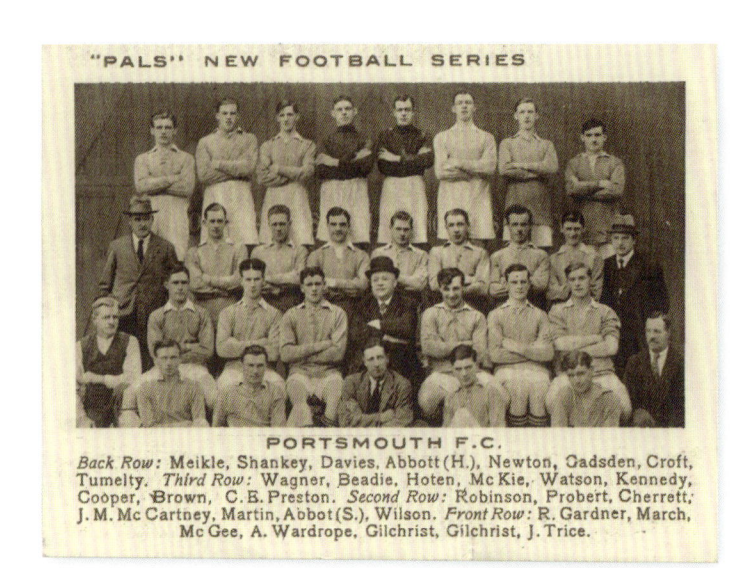

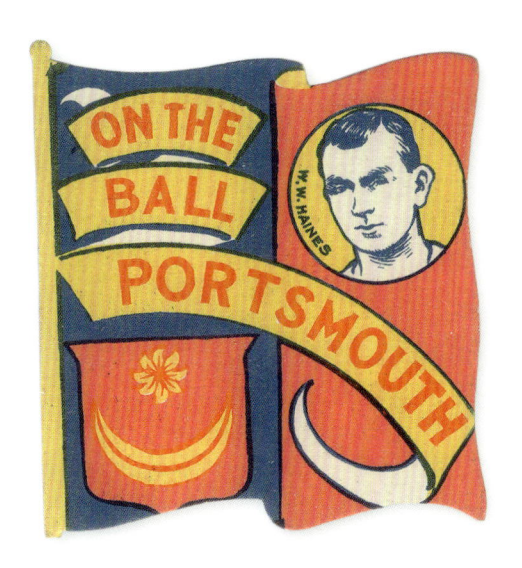

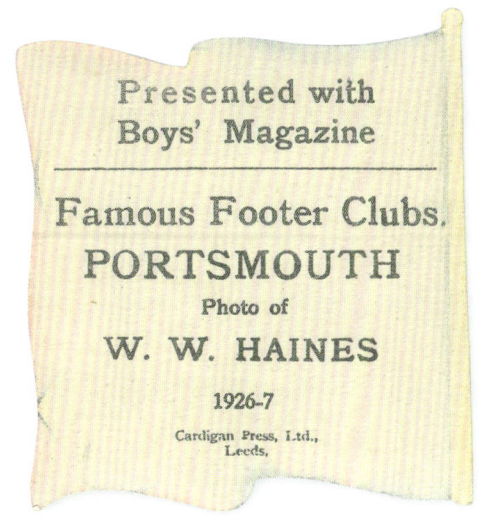

BOYS' MAGAZINE. 1926/27.
Famous Footer Clubs

24 cards. Unnumbered.
Portsmouth/W.W. Haines.
(67 x 60mm).

Boys' Magazine's die-cut *Famous Footer Clubs* cards are similar in style to the earlier Baines shields. Legendary centre-forward Billy 'Farmer's Boy' Haines was recommended to Pompey by a supporter who saw him playing for Frome Town. His four goals in the final game of the 1926/27 season versus Preston North End helped secure promotion to the First Division by the narrowest of margins and took his league tally to 40, a club record that remained unbeaten for 66 years. Haines scored 128 goals in 179 league and cup appearances between 1923 and 1928 before signing for Southampton.

GALLAHER. 1928.

Footballers

100 cards. (Nos. 1–50 – match scenes). No. 27. Aston Villa v Portsmouth. No. 50. Derby County v Portsmouth. (37 x 63mm). (Nos. 51–100 – player portraits). No. 57. Robert Irvine. (63 x 37mm).

Gallaher's series of 100 *Footballers* included both match scenes and player portraits. Pompey were captured in action against Derby County and Aston Villa, while Northern Ireland international Bobby Irvine featured on a portrait card. Signed from Everton in 1928, the inside-forward was known for his clever dribbling skills. Irvine left Pompey two years later to join Welsh side Connah's Quay having made 39 appearances, scoring 11 goals.

The two match scenes also featured in a plain back series of 25 black and white cards, issued by confectionery firm Teasdale the same year.

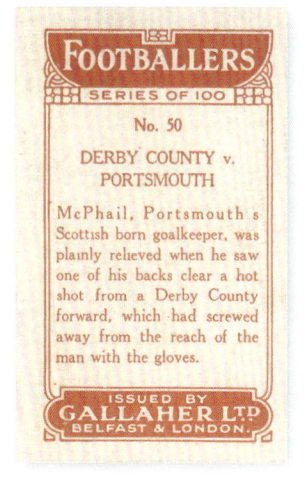

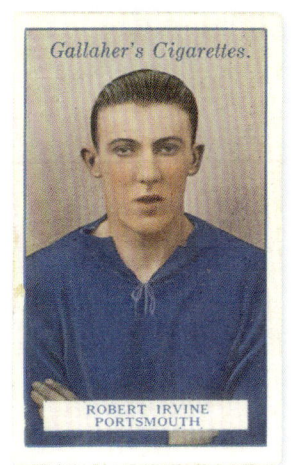

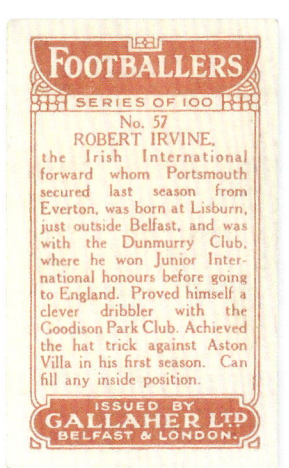

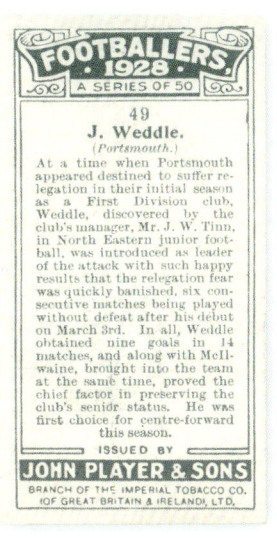

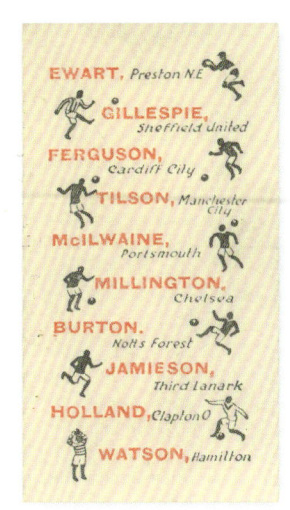

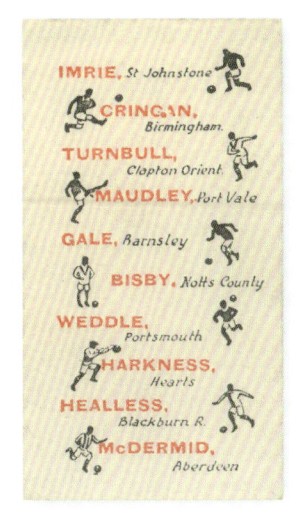

JOHN PLAYER & SONS. 1928.

Footballers 1928

50 cards. No. 49. J. Weddle. (67 x 36mm).

John Player & Sons' 1928 series of 50 illustrated footballers included goal-poacher John Weddle, one of the most famous names in Pompey's history. He arrived as a trialist during the summer of 1927 and went on to become the first-choice centre-forward, replacing Billy Haines. Weddle played in both the 1929 and 1934 FA Cup Final defeats and scored a hat-trick in the 1934 semi-final versus Leicester City, one of seven for the club. He left Pompey in 1938 after 11 seasons at Fratton Park having scored 187 goals in 396 league and cup appearances.

ADVENTURE. 1929.

The Mysto Mind-Reader Football Mystery Cards

10 cards. Unnumbered. McIlwaine, Weddle. (68 x 37mm).

Ten *Mysto Mind-Reader Football Mystery Cards* were given away with Adventure in 1929. Two of the cards feature tiny representations of John McIlwaine and John Weddle.

OGDEN'S. 1926.

Captains of Association Football Clubs, & Colours

44 cards. No. 30. J. Martin.
(67 x 35mm).

BOYS' MAGAZINE. 1929.

Famous Footballers

12 cards. No. 7. John McIlwaine.
(65 x 34mm).

Centre-half John McIlwaine joined a struggling Pompey side from Falkirk in February 1928 for a record £5,000 fee. His defensive qualities ensured relegation to the Second Division was avoided. He was made captain the following season and led the team out for the 1929 FA Cup Final.

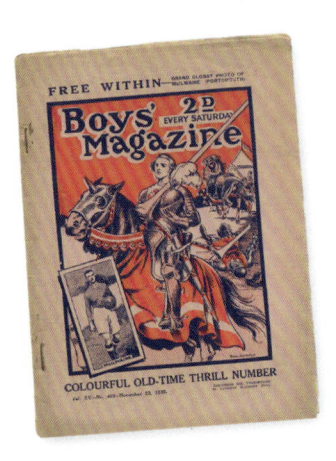

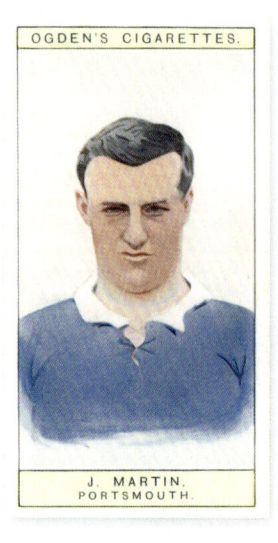

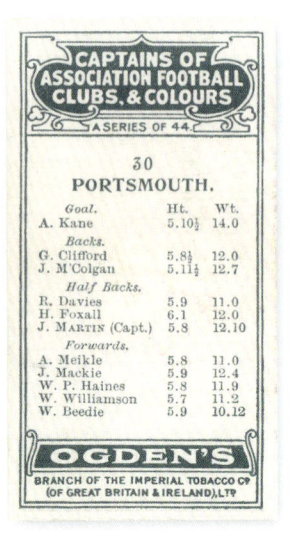

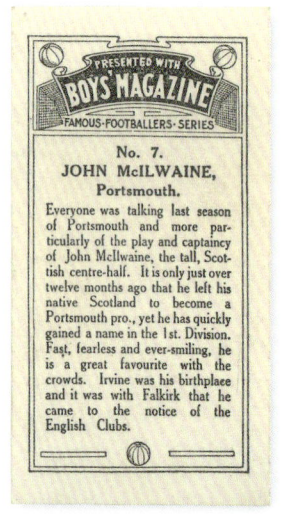

TOPICAL TIMES. 1929.

Footballers

20 cards, issued in pairs. Unnumbered. J. McIlwaine. (44 x 35mm).

Originally issued alongside Ernest Toseland of Manchester City.

THE WIZARD. 1929.

Footballers and Secret Signs

6 metal shields. No. 3. F. Cook/ Tong of Sing Poo. (24 x 20mm).

D.C. Thomson gave away football cards and gifts for several decades with popular titles such as The Wizard, Adventure, The Skipper, The Rover, The Hotspur and Topical Times. The *Footballers and Secret Signs* series of six metal shields, which included Freddie Cook, was issued with The Wizard in 1929. A crowd favourite throughout his Pompey career, Wales international Cook was a member of the promotion-winning side of 1927, and featured in the 1929 FA Cup Final defeat to Bolton Wanderers. An outside-left, he made 268 league and cup appearances between 1926 and 1932, scoring 42 goals.

THIRD TIME LUCKY

A fourth-place finish in 1930/31, followed by eighth-place in 1931/32, suggested Pompey were finding their feet in the First Division. John Weddle and Jimmy Easson, who were proving to be one of the country's finest strike partnerships, each scored more than 20 goals during both seasons.

Pompey continued to make a name for themselves in the FA Cup, reaching Wembley for the second time in 1934. A fine 4-1 semi-final win versus Leicester City at St Andrews saw the team go into the final against Manchester City with hopes high, but as happened five years earlier, an injury to a key player influenced the match. Having lead for the majority of the game by a single goal through Sep Rutherford, Pompey conceded two late goals, the first while Jimmy Allen was off the field receiving treatment with the second coming just two minutes from the end of the game.

By the late 1930s Pompey found themselves battling to retain their top-flight status. Relegation was narrowly avoided in 1937/38 and the following season they again struggled to pull themselves away from the lower reaches of the division. In the FA Cup, however, the team hit a rich vein of form. Four successive home wins, followed by a 2-1 semi-final defeat of Huddersfield Town at Highbury, saw Pompey reach the final for the third time.

Their opponents Wolverhampton Wanderers had finished the season as First Division runners-up and went into the match as clear favourites. Pompey, however, turned the form book on its head, winning 4-1 with an almost faultless display. Two goals from Cliff Parker and one each for Bert Barlow and Jock Anderson meant it was a case of third time lucky and captain Jimmy Guthrie proudly climbed the Wembley steps to collect the trophy from King George VI.

The outbreak of World War Two on 1st September 1939, just three matches into the new season, led to the suspension of competitive football, and Pompey famously held on to the trophy throughout the six long years of hostilities.

1930–1939

BARRATT & CO. 1930/31.

Football Teams 1st Division

66 cards. Unnumbered.
Card 1: Cook, Easson, Kearney (spelt incorrectly on card), Thackeray.
Card 2: Smith, Weddle, Mackie, Forward. *Card 3*: W. Smith, Clifford, Nichol, Gilfillan. (61 x 39mm).

Barratt's *Football Teams 1st Division* series featured three cards of each of the First Division's 22 clubs.

Pompey ended the 1930/31 season in fourth place, their highest league finish until then. Jimmy Easson led the club's goalscoring chart with 29 goals in 42 league games.

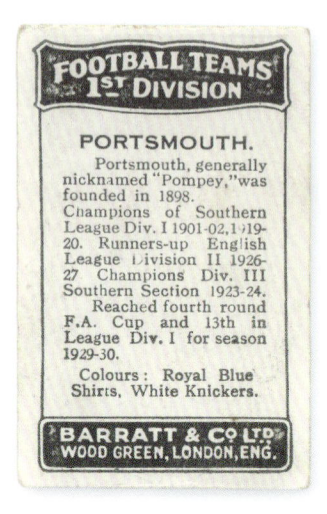

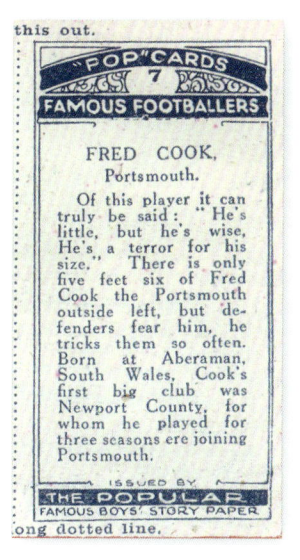

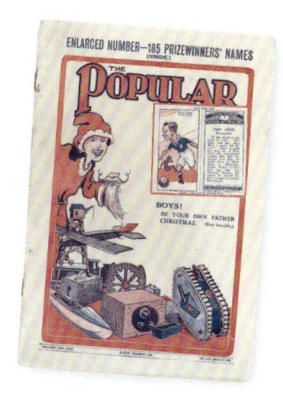

THE POPULAR. 1930.

Famous Footballers "Pop" Cards

12 cut-out cards. No. 7. Fred Cook. (68 x 36mm).

Printed weekly on the front covers of *The Popular* boys' magazine in 1930, this scarce set of caricatures could be trimmed and folded to form cigarette-style cards.

BARRATT & CO. 1930.

Football "Stars"

100 cards. Unnumbered. R. Irvine. (60 x 34mm).

CRESCENT CONFECTIONERY. 1930.

Sportsmen

100 cards. No. 16. J.A. Mackie, No. 17. J. Weddle. (61 x 38mm).

Another extremely rare series issued by Crescent Confectionery, this time featuring 100 sportsmen.

ADVENTURE. 1930.
Footballers and Motor Cars

24 cards. No. 16. J. Easson/Minerva. (68 x 37mm).

TOPICAL TIMES. 1930.
100 Football Stars of 1930

100 paper cut-outs. Unnumbered. J. Easson, J. Gilfillan. (50 x 40mm).

Published as four booklets featuring illustrations and biographies of the top players of the day, including Jimmy Easson and goalkeeper Jock Gilfillan.

THE WIZARD. 1931.
ABC Chart of Football Colours

128 stickers. No. 91. D. Thackeray. (26 x 25mm).

Issued as four sheets of 32 club shirt illustrations. Separate sheets of gummed black and white player portraits could be trimmed and stuck down to complete the images.

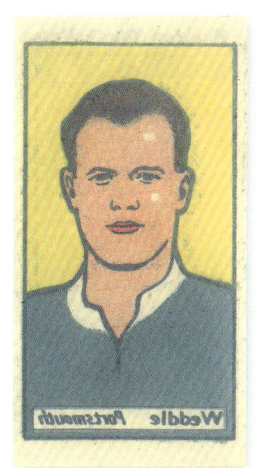

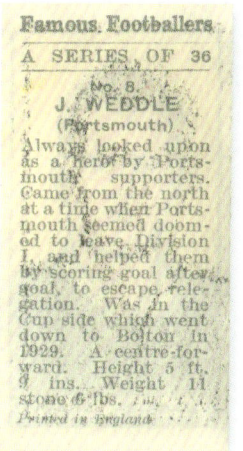

UNKNOWN ISSUER. 1931/32.

Famous Footballers

36 transfers. Image shown flipped as issued. No. 8. J Weddle. (61 x 31mm).

BOY'S CINEMA. 1931.

Football Teams

24 cards. Unnumbered. Portsmouth. (75 x 50mm).

This card features an edited photograph of the 1929 FA Cup Final side. The heads of Tommy Bell, John McIlwaine and David Watson have been replaced with those of William Smith (back row, right), Bob Kearney (middle row, centre) and Jimmy Easson (front row, second from the right).

GODFREY PHILLIPS. 1932–34.

Footballers

137 cards. Unnumbered. Mackie. (65 x 36mm).

These cards were printed directly on to the back of B.D.V. Sports brand cigarette packets. Signed from Arsenal in 1928, Alex Mackie's first season ended in defeat to Bolton Wanderers in the 1929 FA Cup Final. He went on to become a regular in the side and picked up another FA Cup runners-up medal in 1934. Mackie transferred to Northampton Town in 1935 having made 286 league and cup appearances, scoring 2 goals.

LAMBERT & BUTLER. 1931.

Footballers 1930–1

50 cards. No. 20. R. Kearney. (67 x 36mm).

Signed from Dundee in 1928, Bob Kearney replaced John McIlwaine as first-choice centre-half during the 1929/30 season. He made 31 league and cup appearances the following season before, tragically, he was taken seriously ill following an FA Cup Fifth Round match versus West Bromwich Albion and died of pneumonia a week later aged 27.

ADVENTURE/THE ROVER/ THE SKIPPER/THE WIZARD. 1931.

Football Towns and Their Crests/ Famous Ships

32 cards. Unnumbered. Portsmouth/ Aberdeen/Gillingham/Derby/ Satisfaction (1670). (80 x 64mm).

Issued attached to a series of *Famous Ships*, these are usually found cut down to individual cards.

BOYS' MAGAZINE. 1931.

Gallery of Famous Footballers

10 sheets. Unnumbered. F. Cook. (127 x 100mm).

Pompey's Freddie Cook featured in Boys' Magazine's *Gallery of Famous Footballers* series, issued in 1931.

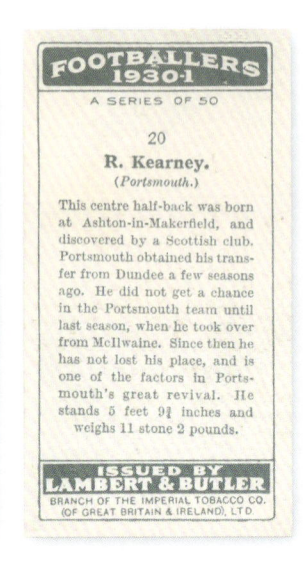

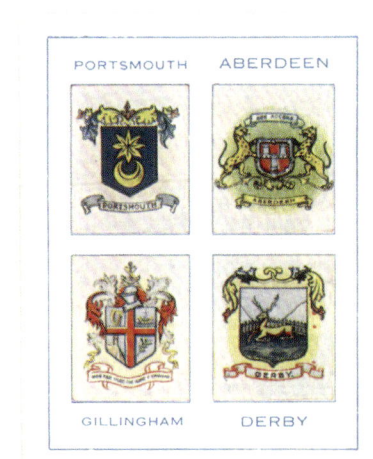

TOPICAL TIMES. 1932.

Star Footballers Panel Portraits

12 cards. Unnumbered.
Jack Smith. (250 x 94mm).

TOPICAL TIMES. 1933.

Star Footballers Panel Portraits

24 cards. Unnumbered.
Fred Worrall. (242 x 88mm).

Predominantly a football periodical, Topical Times was issued weekly between 1919 and 1940. Throughout the 1930s, oversize *Star Footballers Panel Portraits* printed in both colour and black and white were given away with the magazine.

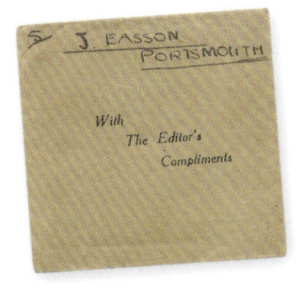

ADVENTURE. 1932.

Star Footballers

14 metal photos. Unnumbered. J. Easson. (64 x 50mm).

These metal photos were prone to being dented, bent and scratched and are rarely found in mint condition.

TEASDALE & CO. 1932.

Footballers

28 known cards. Unnumbered. F. Worrall. (64 x 38mm).

This scarce series, issued by confectionery firm Teasdale, included Pompey's Fred Worrall who is pictured wearing the shirt of Oldham Athletic, his previous club.

OGDEN'S. 1933.

A.F.C. Nicknames

50 cards. No. 36. Portsmouth. (67 x 35mm).

Also issued by Hignett Bros. & Co.

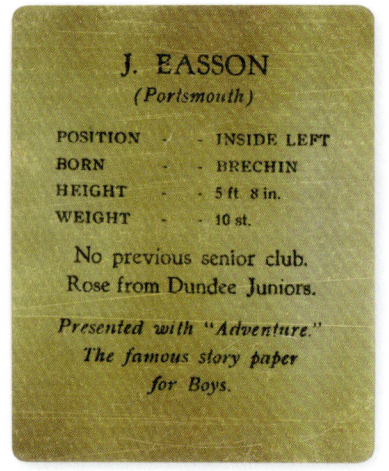

54 | THE OFFICIAL HISTORY OF POMPEY CARDS & STICKERS

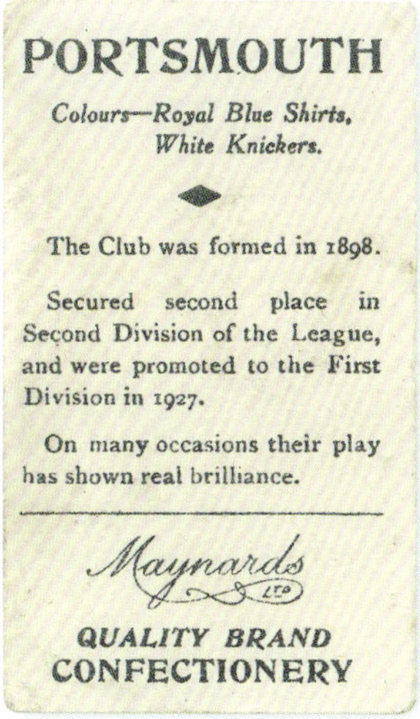

MAYNARDS. 1933.

Football Club Colours

17 known cards. Unnumbered. Portsmouth. (64 x 37mm).

London-based confectionery firm Maynards issued illustrated *Football Club Colours* cards with their products in 1933.

THE CHAMPION. 1933.

The Champion Portfolio of Sport – Soccer's Wily Wizards

8 booklets. Unnumbered. J. Smith, Portsmouth, outside-right. (67 x 47mm).

A collection of eight photographic booklets featuring sporting stars of the day, these were intended to be stuck into an accompanying *Portfolio of Sport* folder. Pompey's Jack Smith was included in the *Soccer's Wily Wizards* booklet alongside Dixie Dean, Peter O'Dowd, E. Blenkinsop, E. Rimmer, Roy Goodall and Alex James.

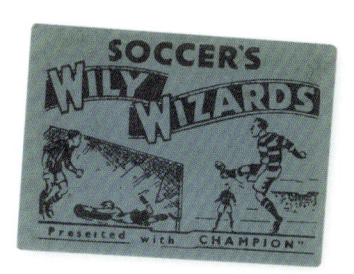

Barratt & Co. issued a series of *Football Team Folders* each season between 1932/33 and 1934/35. Revealing head and shoulders portraits of 12 players when opened, the reverse of each card features a brief history of the club.

BARRATT & CO. 1932/33.

Football Team Folders – English League Division 1.

22 cards. Unnumbered. J. Weddle, J. Allen, F. Worrall, J. Gilfillan, F. Cook, D. Thackeray, W. Smith, J. Mackie, J. Nichol, J. Easson, J. Smith, W. Rochford. (60 x 79mm).

BARRATT & CO. 1933/34.

Football Team Folders – English League Division 1.

22 cards. Unnumbered. J. Smith, J. Gilfillan, S. Rutherford, J. Allen, J. Easson, F. Worrall, J. Nichol, W. Rochford, J. Mackie, J. Weddle, D. Thackeray, W. Smith. (60 x 79mm).

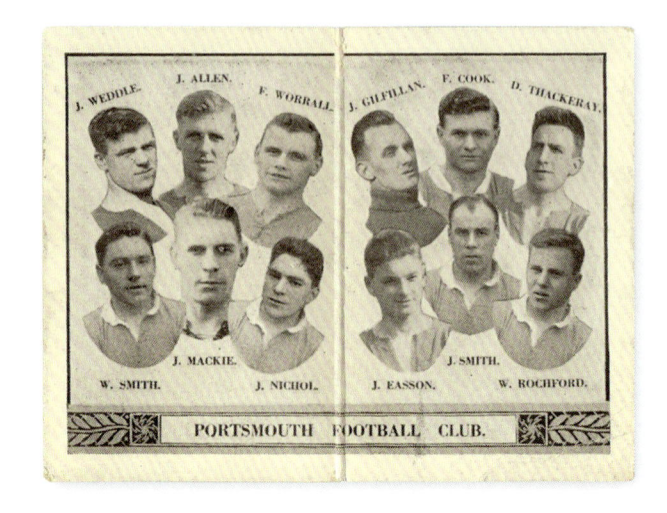

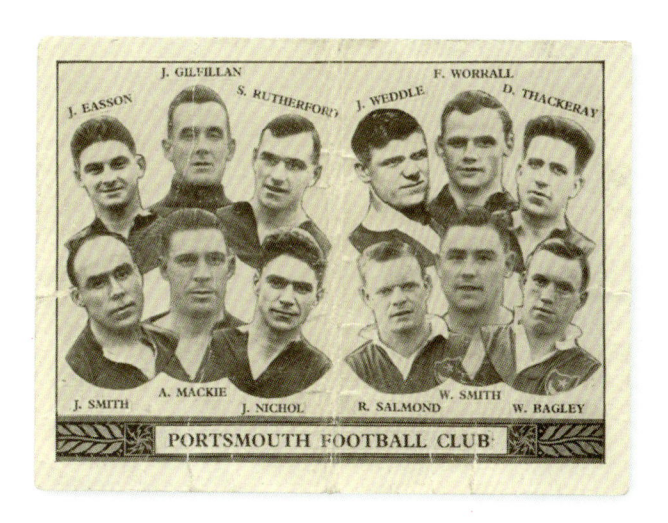

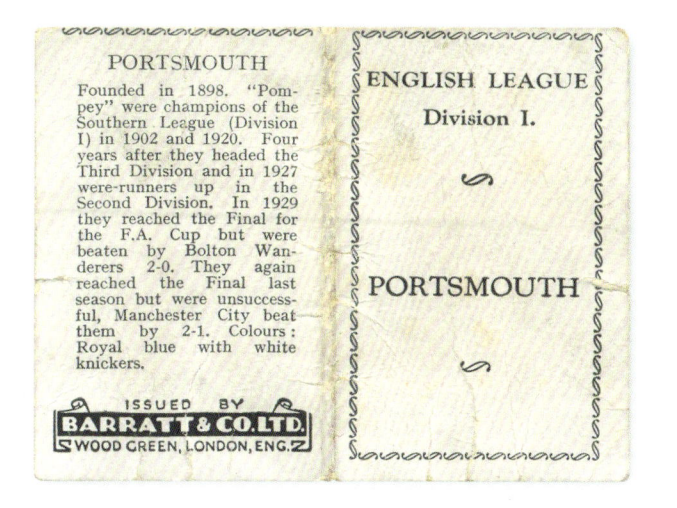

BARRATT & CO. 1934/35.

Football Team Folders – English League Division 1.

22 cards. Unnumbered. J. Easson, J. Gilfillan, S. Rutherford, J. Weddle, F. Worrall, D. Thackeray, J. Smith, A. Mackie, J. Nichol, R. Salmond, W. Smith, W. Bagley. (60 x 79mm).

Brothers Jack and William Smith featured on all three Portsmouth folders. Jack, an inside-right, scored in the 1-0 FA Cup Semi-Final win versus Aston Villa at Highbury in 1929 and represented England on three occasions in 1931. He spent almost seven years at Fratton Park, making 290 appearances, before losing his place to Dave Thackeray and transferring to Bournemouth in 1935.

Left-back William joined Pompey in 1928, six months after Jack. A reliable performer, he missed only four games between 1930/31 and 1936/37. Both Jack and William played in Pompey's FA Cup Final defeat to Manchester City in 1934.

UNKNOWN ISSUER. 1932/33.
'Red Star' Footballers
31 transfers. Image shown flipped as issued. Unnumbered. Weddle. (32 x 38mm).

ADVENTURE/THE SKIPPER/ THE ROVER/THE WIZARD. 1933.
Football Teams
64 cards. No. 48. Portsmouth. (43 x 31mm).

THE SKIPPER. 1934.
The Winner Football Flags
63 flags. Unnumbered. J. Weddle/ Portsmouth. (22 x 29mm).

Issued as three sheets of 21 flags to be cut out, folded around a pin and placed into an accompanying album.

ADVENTURE. 1936.
Football Stamp Album
129 paper stamps. No. 16. Portsmouth. (29 x 22mm).

ADVENTURE. 1934.
Hunt the Cup
52 cards. No. 20. J. Weddle/The City. (44 x 31mm).

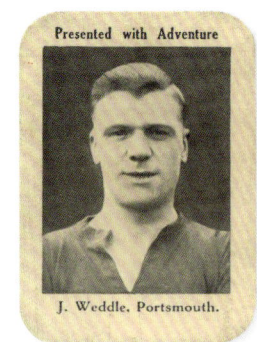

58 | THE OFFICIAL HISTORY OF POMPEY CARDS & STICKERS

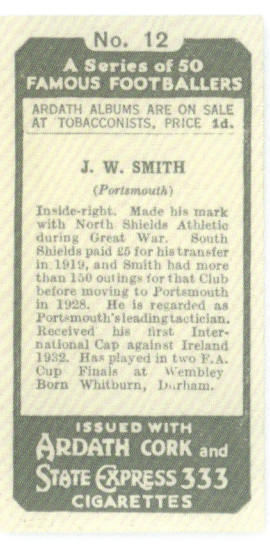

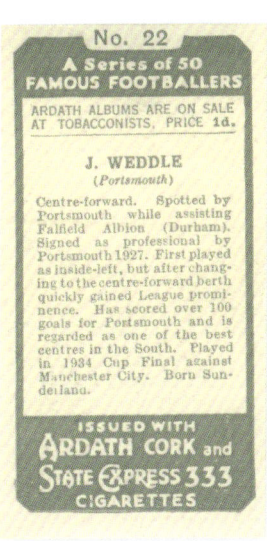

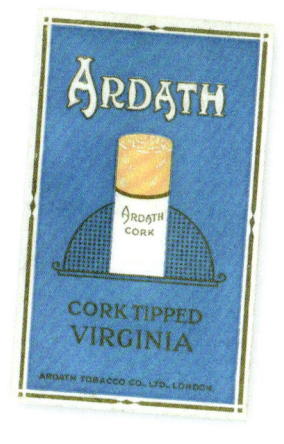

ARDATH. 1934.

Famous Footballers

50 cards. No. 12. J.W. Smith, No. 22. J. Weddle. (68 x 35mm).

The 'sticky back' card was an innovation introduced during the 1930s. An adhesive applied to the reverse during production allowed collectors to stick their cards into albums with ease. One of the first sticky back collections to be issued was Ardath's 1934 series of *Famous Footballers*, featuring Pompey's Jack Smith and John Weddle.

CARRERAS. 1934.

Footballers (small titles)

75 cards. No. 29. J. Nichol, No. 43. J. Gilfillan, No. 50. J. Smith, No. 67. J. Weddle. (68 x 36mm).

Carreras' series of 75 *Footballers* was issued twice in quick succession with different artwork. The first printing featured coloured photographs and small titles, the second was updated to painted portraits and large titles.

Right-half Jimmy Nichol joined from Gillingham in 1927. He made 383 league and cup appearances, scoring nine goals, before returning to his former club in 1937. After the war Nichol returned to Fratton Park, taking up the position of head trainer.

Goalkeeper Jock Gilfillan signed from Heart of Midlothian in 1928 and served Pompey for eight years. He made 360 appearances before losing his place to George Strong and joined Queens Park Rangers in June 1937.

Nichol, Gilfillan, Smith and Weddle all featured in the 2-1 FA Cup Final defeat to Manchester City the year this series was issued.

CARRERAS. 1934.

Footballers (large titles)

75 cards. No. 29. J. Nichol, No. 43. J. Gilfillan, No. 50. J. Smith, No. 67. J. Weddle. (68 x 36mm).

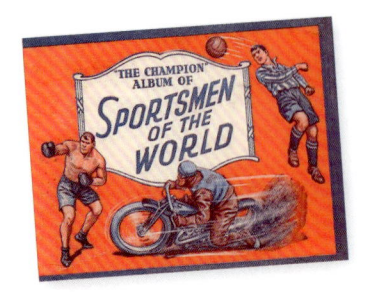

THE CHAMPION. 1934.

*Sportsmen of the World –
Football Cup-Final Captains*

32 cards. Unnumbered.
D. Thackeray. (69 x 37mm).

The *Sportsmen of the World* album included the 1934 FA Cup Final captains, Pompey's Dave Thackeray and Sam Cowan of Manchester City.

Left-half Thackeray signed from Motherwell in 1928 and made over 300 league and cup appearances during his eight-year stay at Fratton Park. In 1950 he returned to take up the position of assistant groundsman.

JOHN SINCLAIR. 1935.

English & Scottish Football Stars

50 cards. No. 48. D. Thackeray.
(66 x 34mm).

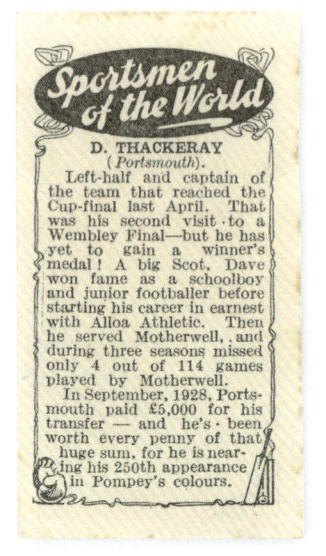

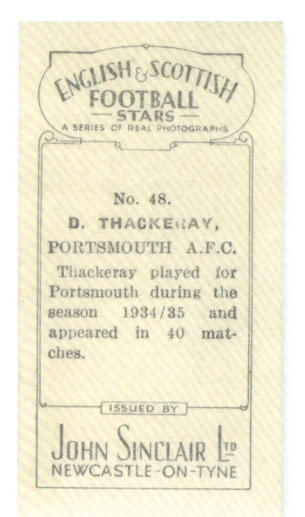

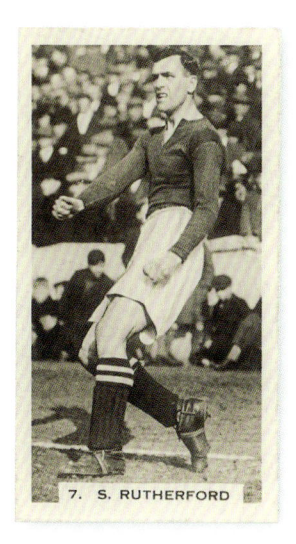

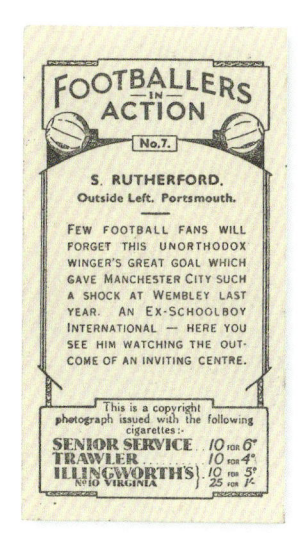

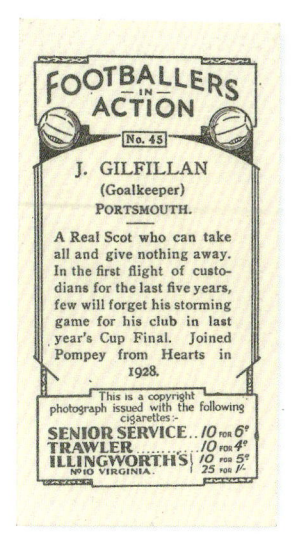

J.A. PATTREIOUEX. 1935.

Footballers in Action

78 cards. No. 7. S. Rutherford, No. 45. J. Gilfillan. (67 x 34mm).

J.A. Pattreiouex's *Footballers in Action* series featured outside-left Sep Rutherford and goalkeeper Jock Gilfillan, both members of the 1934 FA Cup Final side. Rutherford, the goalscorer in the 2-1 defeat, joined Pompey from Blyth Spartans in 1927 but due to the form of Freddie Cook, had to wait five years before he became a regular in Pompey's side. Rutherford joined Blackburn Rovers in 1936 having made 130 league and cup appearances, scoring 37 goals.

W.D. & H.O. WILLS. 1935.

Association Footballers

50 cards. No. 49. F. Worrall.
(68 x 35mm).

This series was also issued in the Channel Islands, with the album offer details and Imperial Tobacco Co. information omitted from the reverse of the cards.

GODFREY PHILLIPS. 1936.

Soccer Stars

50 cards. No. 8. F. Worrall,
No. 18. J. Easson. (67 x 36mm).

CARRERAS. 1936.

Popular Footballers

48 cards. No. 37. F. Worrall.
(68 x 35mm).

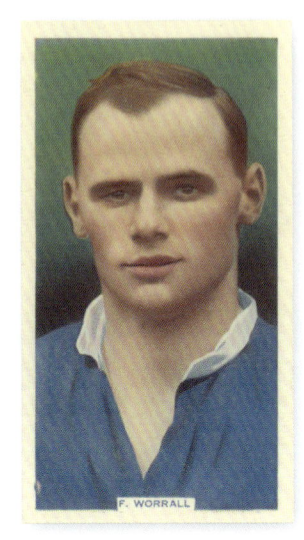

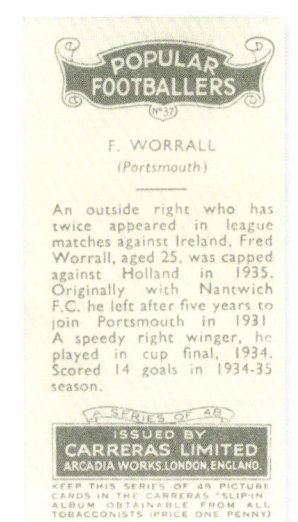

TOPICAL TIMES. 1935.

Star Footballers Panel Portraits

28 cards. Unnumbered.
Bob Salmond. (250 x 94mm).

TOPICAL TIMES. 1936.

Star Footballers Panel Portraits

16 cards. Unnumbered.
Clifford Parker. (250 x 94mm).

Cliff Parker's Pompey career spanned 12 seasons either side of World War Two. He made his debut on Boxing Day 1933 and was soon first-choice for the outside-left position from which he regularly set up goals with pinpoint crosses. He picked up an FA Cup winners' medal in 1939, scoring two goals in the 4-1 victory. Remarkably, in his late-30s, Parker also appeared in both the championship-winning sides of 1948/49 and 1949/50. He made a total of 256 appearances between 1933 and 1951, scoring 63 goals.

CARRERAS. 1935.

Famous Footballers

48 cards. No. 7. D. Thackeray, No. 33. J. Weddle (first printing), No. 33. J. Weddle (redrawn, second printing). (68 x 35mm).

Card numbers 25-48 in this series, including no. 33 John Weddle, were redrawn and reissued.

GODFREY PHILLIPS. 1936.

Famous Footballers

50 cards. No. 18. J. Easson. (67 x 36mm).

Inside-left Jimmy Easson signed in 1929 and proved to be a potent striker, scoring over 100 goals during 10 years in Pompey's colours. Thirty goals in 45 league and cup appearances in 1930/31 were followed by 24 in 45 games the following season. He appeared in the 1934 FA Cup Final defeat before a loss of form led to a transfer to Fulham in 1939. He maintained his connections with Pompey after World War Two, serving as assistant trainer during the championship seasons. Identical cards were issued with both the *International Caps* and *Soccer Stars* series in 1936.

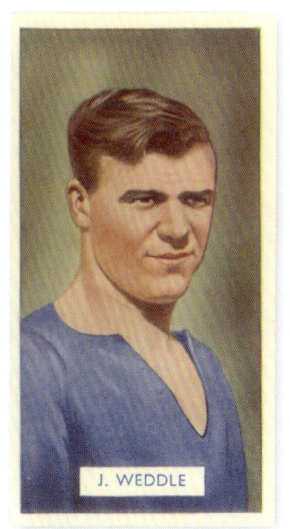

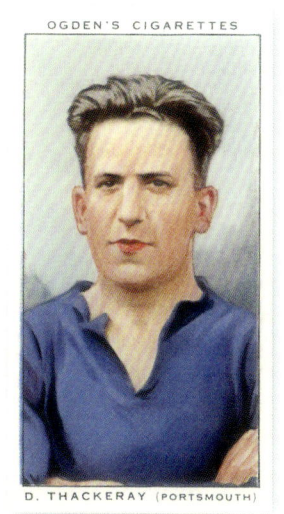

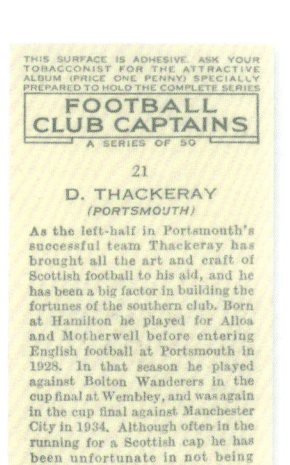

OGDEN'S. 1936.

Football Club Captains

50 cards. No. 21. D. Thackeray. (67 x 35mm).

Also issued by Hignett Bros. & Co.

GODFREY PHILLIPS. 1937.

Spot the Winner

50 cards. No. 26. F. Worrall (spelt incorrectly on card). (67 x 36mm).

Outside-right Fred Worrall was well-known for his superstitious nature. During the 1939 FA Cup Final he kept a small horseshoe in his pocket, placed a sprig of heather inside each sock, tied a white elephant charm to one of his garters and put a lucky sixpence in his boot. He also insisted on fastening manager Jack Tinn's 'lucky' spats before each match in the competition. Signed from Oldham Athletic, Worrall made 338 appearances between 1931 and 1939, scoring 71 goals. This series can also be found with the reverse inverted.

THE CHAMPION. 1935.

Autographs

100 autographs. Unnumbered.
John Weddle. (42 x 82mm).

John Weddle was one of 100 stars included in The Champion's album of *Autographs* which featured personalities of the day. Facsimile signatures could be cut out and stuck into position next to the corresponding portrait.

THE CHAMPION. 1937.

The "Champion" Album of Famous Footballers' Autographs and Photographs

80 autographs. Unnumbered.
J.F. Easson, J. Gilfillan.

Another autograph album given away with The Champion, this time featuring famous footballers.

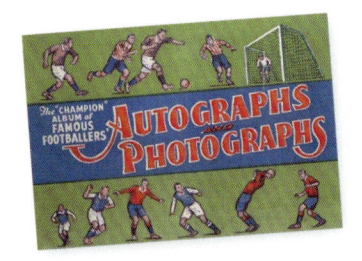

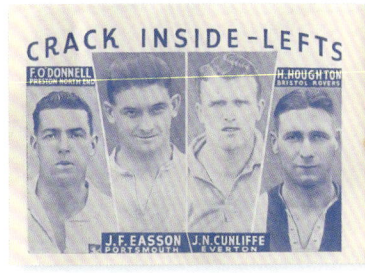

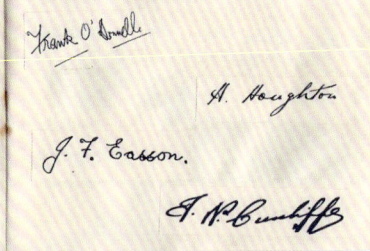

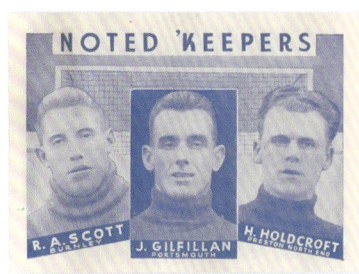

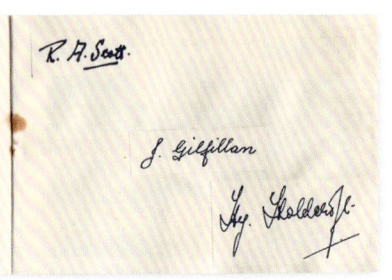

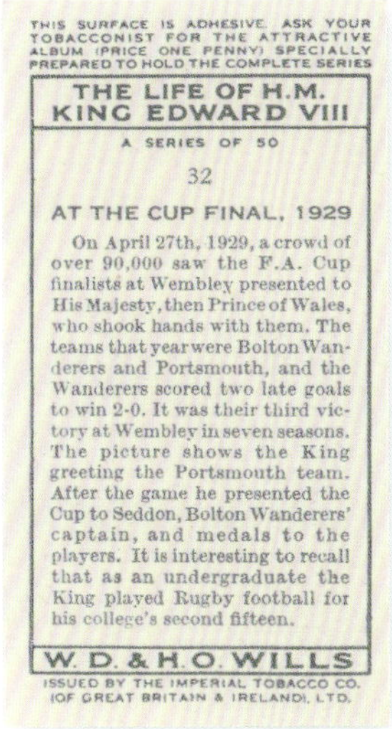

W.D. & H.O. WILLS. 1937.

The Life of H.M. King Edward VIII

50 cards. No. 32. At The Cup Final, 1929. (68 x 36mm).

Produced to coincide with the coronation of Edward VIII, this series was destroyed when he abdicated the throne in 1936, although some sets did survive. His Majesty, then the Prince of Wales, is shown greeting the Portsmouth team ahead of the FA Cup Final defeat to Bolton Wanderers in 1929.

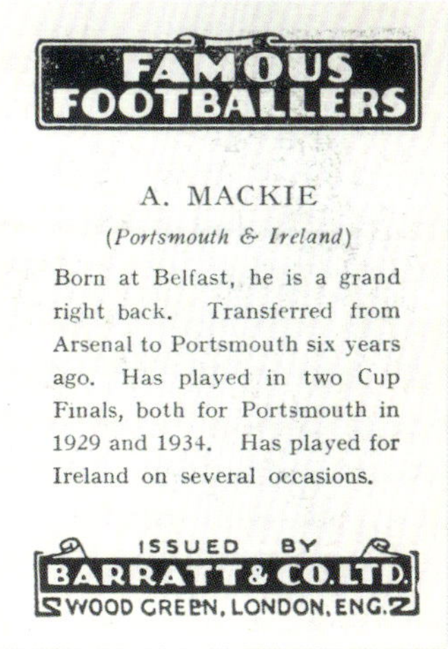

BARRATT & CO. 1935/36.

Famous Footballers

100 cards. Unnumbered. A. Mackie. (62 x 44mm).

Alex Mackie featured in the first of Barratt's long-running annual *Famous Footballers* series, issued with packets of sweet cigarettes during the 1935/36 season.

TOPICAL TIMES. 1937.
Triple Panel Portraits

8 cards. Unnumbered. George J. Strong, Portsmouth F.C. (250 x 200mm).

In addition to individual varieties, *Triple Panel Portraits* were given away with Topical Times magazine.

Goalkeeper George Strong signed from Chesterfield in 1935 and made his Pompey debut in December 1936. Following 61 league and cup appearances, his place was taken by Harry Walker and he moved to Gillingham in August 1938. Strong guested for Burnley during World War Two and signed for the Turf Moor club in 1946. He went on to play 244 league games during his spell in Lancashire which included a club-record 203 consecutive appearances between 1946 and 1951.

TOPICAL TIMES. 1937.

Miniature Panel Portraits of Football Stars

24 cards. Unnumbered. W.M. Bagley. (125 x 46mm).

Small *Panel Portraits* were issued across two series in 1937 and 1938. Bill Bagley played in four rounds during the 1938/39 cup run and was unlucky to lose his place to Bert Barlow for the semi-final and final. He did, however, receive a winners' medal having been selected as first reserve.

TOPICAL TIMES. 1938.

Stars of To-Day

24 cards. Unnumbered. Lewis Morgan. (125 x 46mm).

Signed from Dundee in 1935, Lew Morgan was a regular at right-back between 1937 and 1939 and played in the 1939 FA Cup Final. He transferred to Watford after the war before joining non-league Chelmsford City in 1948.

BARRATT & CO. 1939/40.

Famous Footballers

110 cards. No. 7. H. Barlow, No. 10. J. Beattie. (62 x 44mm).

Bert Barlow, pictured wearing a Wolverhampton Wanderers shirt, signed for Pompey just two months before scoring the opening goal in the FA Cup Final victory against his old side in 1939. He continued to play for Pompey during the war and went on to score nine goals in 31 league appearances during the championship campaigns of 1948/49 and 1949/50.

Centre-forward James Beattie proved to be an adequate replacement for the legendary John Weddle when he signed from St. Johnstone in February 1937. He scored 21 goals in 38 league and cup matches in 1937/38 before injury and illness kept him out of the side from December into the New Year the following season. Jock Anderson took his place and following just one more appearance, Beattie joined Millwall in the summer of 1939.

KLENE – VAL "FOOTER" GUM. 1938/39.
Footballers

50 cards. No. 18. R. Salmond.
(70 x 60mm).

Dutch confectionery firm Klene issued a series of 50 British *Footballers* with packets of Val "Footer" Gum in 1938/39. Bob Salmond joined Pompey in 1930, but was kept out of the side by the form of Jimmy Allen. When Allen moved to Aston Villa in 1934, his departure paved the way for Salmond to make the centre-half position his own. He was appointed club captain at the start of the 1937/38 season but an injury sustained after only six games allowed Tommy Rowe to take his place. Salmond joined Chelsea in November 1938.

TOPICAL TIMES. 1939.
Album of Great Players – Close-ups of the Stars

24 cards. Unnumbered. G. Walker.
(76 x 60mm).

Goalkeeper Harry Walker signed for Pompey in 1938 and made two important saves the following year in the FA Cup Final win. He also played regularly for the club in the Wartime League while working at Portsmouth Dockyard. Walker made a total of 55 appearances before switching to Nottingham Forest in 1947.

W.A. & A.C. CHURCHMAN. 1938.

*Association Footballers
(First Series)*

50 cards. No. 49. F. Worrall. (67 x 35mm).

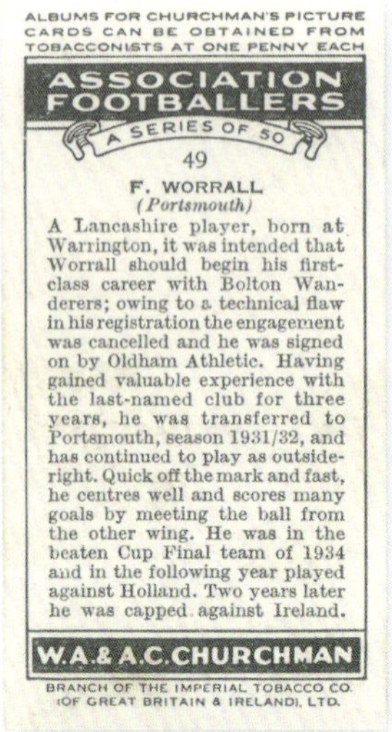

W.A. & A.C. CHURCHMAN. 1939.

*Association Footballers
(Second Series)*

50 cards. No. 40. T. Rowe. (67 x 35mm).

Tommy Rowe joined Pompey in 1934 but it wasn't until the 1937/38 season that he became a regular in the side. He appeared in all the rounds during the 1938/39 FA Cup campaign including the final when he played at centre-half.

While serving in the Royal Air Force as a bomber pilot during World War Two, Rowe's aircraft was shot down over Germany and, having successfully parachuted out, he was held as a Prisoner of War for 14 months. He was awarded the Distinguished Flying Cross in 1943.

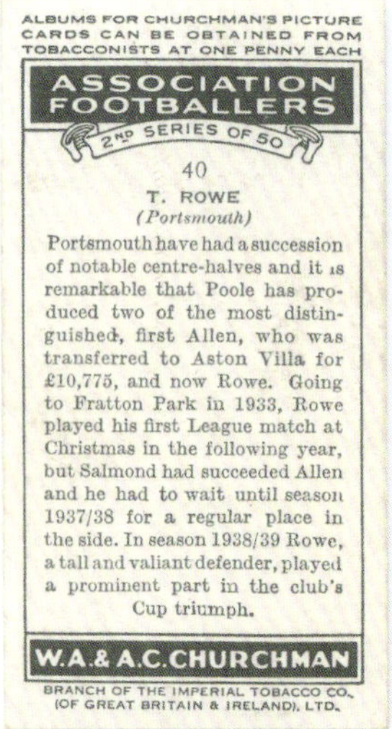

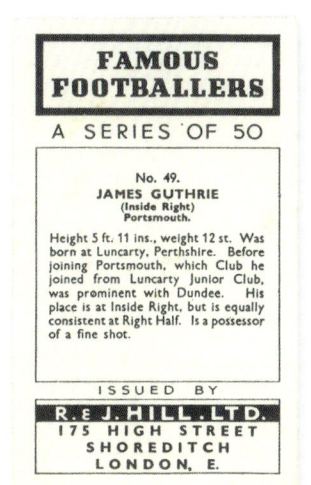

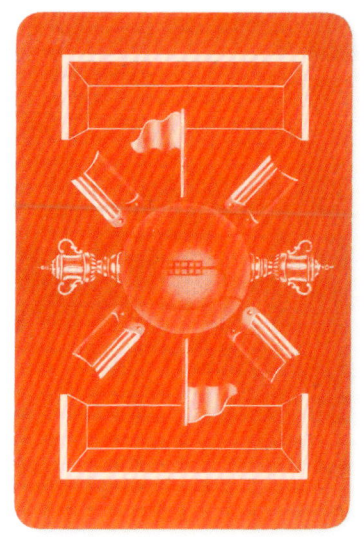

R. & J. HILL. 1939.

Famous Footballers

50 + 25 additional cards.
No. 49. J. Guthrie. (63 x 38mm).

Captain Jimmy Guthrie was presented with the FA Cup by King George VI on behalf of his victorious side the year this series was issued. He also led Pompey out at Wembley for a second time three years later ahead of the 2-0 defeat to Brentford in the London War Cup Final of 1942. The original set of 50 cards can be found with two different addresses on the reverse.

PEPYS. 1939/40.

"It's a Goal" (First Edition)

44 cards. Unnumbered.
Portsmouth. (88 x 57mm).

A card game including the First and Second Division clubs of the 1939/40 season, the box features an illustration of Jock Anderson's goal in the 1939 FA Cup Final which put Pompey 2-0 up just before half-time.

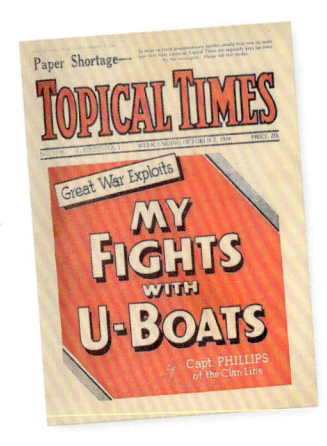

TOPICAL TIMES. 1938.

Star Footballers Panel Portraits

14 cards. Unnumbered.
James F. Beattie. (250 x 94mm).

TOPICAL TIMES. 1939.

Star Footballers Panel Portraits

16 cards. Unnumbered.
Thomas Rowe. (250 x 94mm).

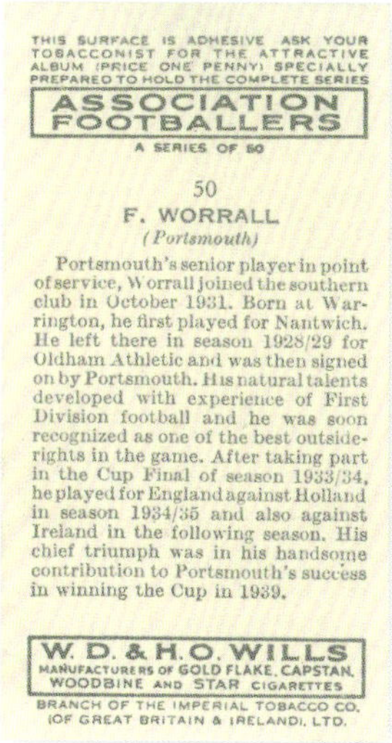

W.D. & H.O. WILLS. 1939.

Association Footballers

50 cards. No. 50. F. Worrall. (68 x 35mm).

This series was also issued in Ireland with a non-adhesive back.

SHERMAN'S POOLS LTD. 1938/39.

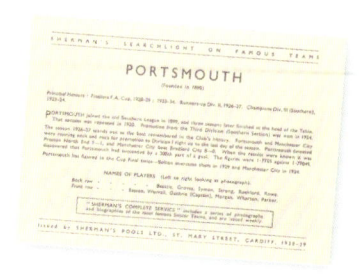

Sherman's Searchlight on Famous Teams

37 cards. Unnumbered. Portsmouth. (100 x 140mm).

A series of photographic team cards issued by Sherman's Pools, a Cardiff-based football pools promoter, throughout the 1938/39 season.

BACK-TO-BACK CHAMPIONS

When league football resumed in 1946, Pompey's FA Cup-winning side had been dismantled, with several members of the squad being replaced by wartime discoveries. Following a mid-table finish in 1946/47, Jack Tinn announced his retirement and was replaced by chief scout Bob Jackson.

Jackson's first season in charge saw Pompey finish in eighth position and, as the club kicked off their Golden Jubilee celebrations in 1948/49, hopes were high that his side would be capable of challenging for the league title. With an impressive unbeaten record of 18 wins and three draws at Fratton Park, supplemented by some big wins away from home, Pompey lived up to expectation and clinched the title with three games to spare.

In the FA Cup, Pompey's chances of securing the first league and cup double since Aston Villa achieved the feat in 1897 sadly evaporated with a disappointing 3-1 semi-final defeat to Second Division Leicester City at Highbury.

During the 1949/50 season Pompey struggled to find the consistency of the previous campaign and were made to wait until the final game to claim their second title. Needing a win against Aston Villa, who were duly beaten 5-1, Pompey's impressive defensive record of only 38 goals conceded in 42 matches proved decisive in winning the championship with a goal average of 1.947 to second place Wolverhampton Wanderers' 1.551.

Under the leadership of Eddie Lever in 1954/55, Pompey's third-place finish was as close as the team came to emulating the championship sides' success. The failure to replace some of the ageing star players saw the side's form suffer and after narrowly avoiding relegation in 1957/58, Lever was dismissed, with Freddie Cox taking his place.

Cox, however, failed to stop the rot. Having managed just six league wins, Pompey finished the season rock-bottom, and relegation brought their 32-year stay in the First Division to an end.

1940–1959

BIRMINGHAM EVENING GAZETTE. 1946/47.

These Are Soccer Stars (New Series)

65 known paper cut-outs. No. 20. G. Wharton, No. 31. Herbert Barlow, No. 33. Jimmy McAlinden. (203 x 47mm).

A series of cut-outs that included three Pompey players was printed in the Birmingham Evening Gazette throughout the 1946/47 season.

Guy Wharton joined Pompey from Wolverhampton Wanderers in 1937 and immediately slotted in at left-half. He played in the 1939 FA Cup Final before serving as a sergeant instructor in the Royal Tank Regiment during World War Two. Wharton lost his place in the side to Jimmy Scoular during the 1946/47 season and transferred to Darlington in 1948.

SUNDAY DISPATCH. 1947.

Football League Stars

20 paper cut-outs. No. 18. Reg Flewin. (132 x 46mm).

Reg Flewin made his Pompey debut in April 1939 before serving in the Royal Marines during World War Two. He was based locally during the hostilities and appeared regularly in Pompey's wartime side. In 1946 he was appointed captain and led the side through both championship campaigns.

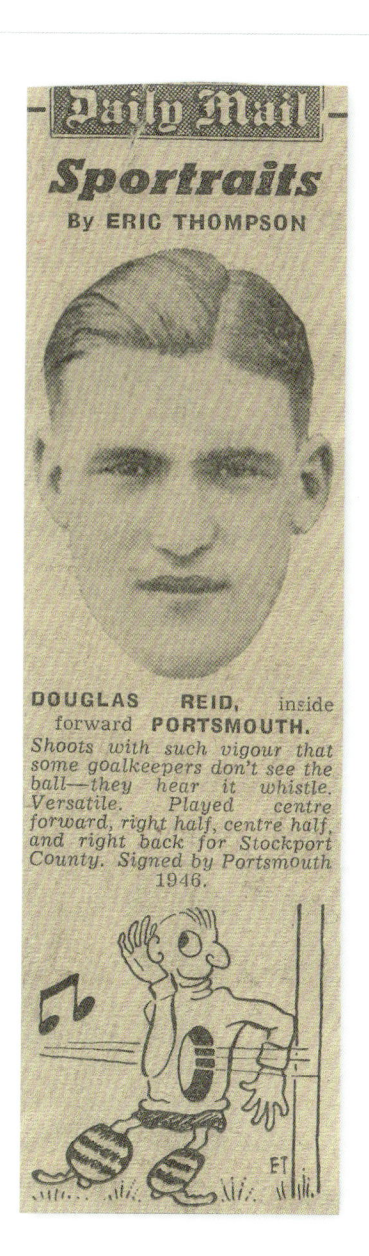

DAILY GRAPHIC. 1946/47.

Star Pictures of Players

121 known paper cut-outs. Unnumbered. Butler, Ferrier, Rookes, Dickinson, Flewin, Scoular, Parker, Barlow, McAlinden, Froggatt, Reid. (30 x 25mm).

Printed daily in the Daily Graphic newspaper featuring teams from the First and Second divisions. Eleven of these tiny portraits were issued per club.

DAILY MAIL. 1947/48.

Sportraits

50 paper cut-outs. Unnumbered. Douglas Reid. (235 x 94mm).

The Daily Mail's series of 50 *Sportraits* was printed throughout the 1947/48 season. Each included a photographic portrait, brief biography and cartoon.

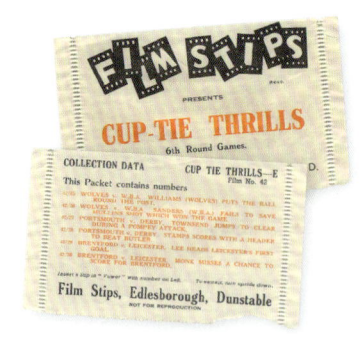

FILM STIPS. 1948/49.
Cup-Tie Thrills

54 stips. *Packet B:* No. 42 - 11. Portsmouth v Newport. Butler swings on the crossbar after clearing. *Packet C:* No. 42 - 17. Portsmouth v Newport. Grant jumps to save from Phillips. *Packet E:* No. 42 - 27. Portsmouth v Derby. Townsend jumps to clear during a Portsmouth attack, No. 42 - 28. Portsmouth v Derby. Stamps scores with a header to beat Butler. (35 x 19mm).

Film Stips were sold in packets of strips of 35mm film or six individual frames. Featuring notable events of the day, they could be viewed through a Cine 'Vuwer', or a Stip Master Projector.

The 1948/49 FA Cup competition was captured in a series of 54 stips titled *Cup-Tie Thrills*. Pompey's 5th Round tie with Newport County and the 6th Round win versus Derby County, which set Fratton Park's attendance record of 51,385, were featured in Packets B, C and E.

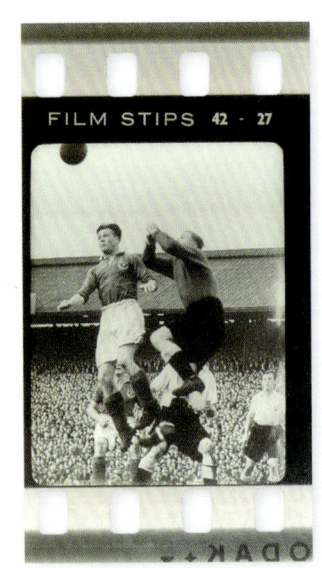

Packet F: No. 42 - 31. Leicester score their first goal through Revie, No. 42 - 32. Portsmouth equalise after 25 minutes through Harris, No. 42 - 33. Chisholm scores Leicester's second goal, No. 42 - 34. Butler misses ball, Revie dashes and scores third goal, No. 42 - 35. A shot from the Leicester forwards goes wide, No. 42 - 36. McGraw leaps to save a shot from the Portsmouth forwards. (19 x 35mm).

The FA Cup Semi-Final against Leicester City at Highbury featured in Packet F. Pompey's solitary goal, an equaliser through Peter Harris, was the only highlight of the 3-1 defeat.

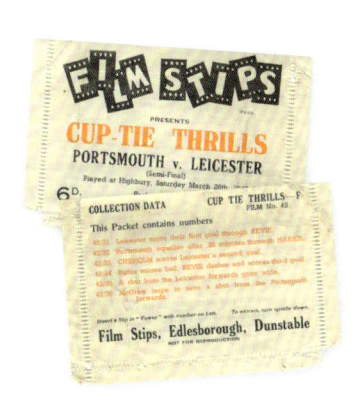

A. & J. DONALDSON. 1948.

Sports Favourites

500 cards. No. 130. D. Reid, No. 389. J. Dickinson. (63 x 39mm).

A. & J. Donaldson's series of *Sports Favourites* was distributed in booklets of eight or nine cards.

Alton-born left-half Jimmy Dickinson needs little, if any, introduction. The greatest servant Pompey has ever had, 'Gentleman Jim' played a club-record 764 league games, 845 in all, and represented England 48 times, including three appearances at each of the World Cup Finals in 1950 and 1954. He served Pompey as a player between 1946 and 1965, then as public relations officer and club secretary, before accepting the position of manager in May 1977.

Following a 1-1 draw at Oakwell versus Barnsley in March 1979, Dickinson suffered a heart attack and he was asked to resign by the Pompey board at the end of the season. He recovered sufficiently to become chief executive but suffered a second heart attack in September 1982 and died suddenly two months later at home in Alton aged 57.

Dickinson's image has featured among the seating in the Fratton End stand since its construction in 1997.

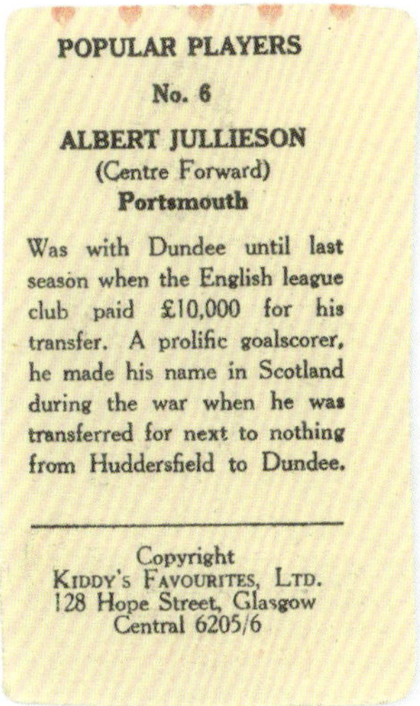

KIDDY'S FAVOURITES. 1948.

Popular Players

52 cards. No. 6. Albert Juliussen (spelt incorrectly on card). (66 x 39mm).

Kiddy's Favourites' stapled booklets of *Popular Players* cards, issued in 1948, included centre-forward Albert Juliussen who joined Pompey from Dundee in 1947. He played only seven games, scoring four goals, before being sold to Everton who paid a record £10,500 fee to secure his services.

BARRATT & CO. AND NAPRO. 1949.

Famous Footballers and Stars of Soccer

40 transfers. Images shown flipped as issued. Unnumbered. J. Dickinson, R. Flewin. (58 x 35mm).

Sheets of *Famous Footballers* and *Stars of Soccer* transfers were issued in Christmas stockings along with a selection of sweets and gifts in 1949.

1940–1959 | 85

CHADA S.A. (CHICLES TABAY). 1948–49.

Album Deportivo – Reportajes Fotograficas Tabay

234 cards. No. A - 197. Reg Flewin. (50 x 30mm).

An album of sporting highlights, issued in Spain by gum manufacturer Chicles Tabay. Captain Reg Flewin is shown cutting the Golden Jubilee cake in the Fratton Park boardroom following an impressive 4-1 victory over reigning league champions Arsenal on 27th November 1948.

L.T.A. ROBINSON. 1949.

Football Stars of Today and Tomorrow

44 paper cut-outs. Unnumbered. Jimmy Dickinson. (84 x 55mm).

Meet the Soccer Stars

44 paper cut-outs. Unnumbered. Peter Harris. (84 x 55mm).

L.T.A. Robinson published two booklets of footballers in 1949. Each page featured several framed action shots that could be cut down to individual cards, complete with detailed biographies on the reverse.

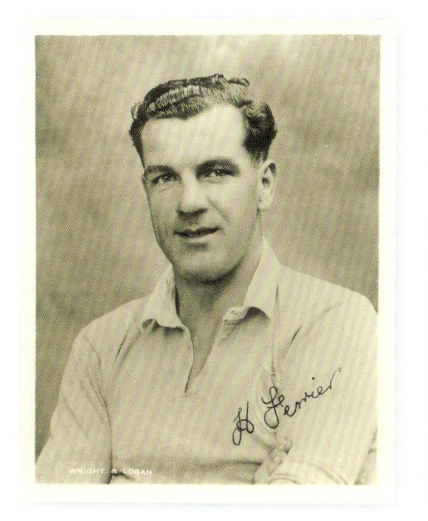

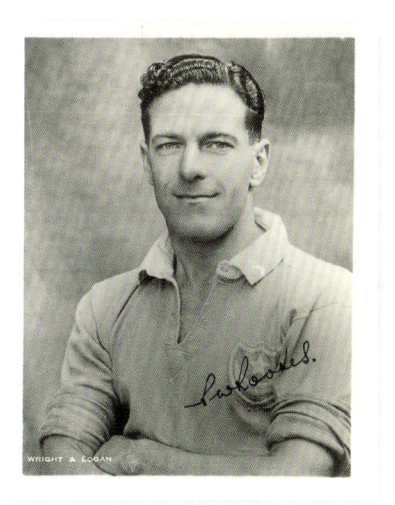

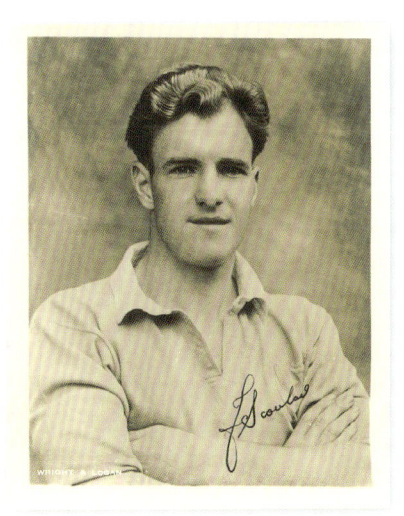

WRIGHT & LOGAN. 1948/49.
Portsmouth F.C. Footballers

11 cards. Unnumbered. B. Barlow, E. Butler, J. Dickinson, H. Ferrier, R. Flewin, J. Froggatt, P. Harris, L. Phillips, D. Reid, P. Rookes, J. Scoular. (88 x 68mm).

Commercial photographers Wright & Logan of Southsea produced a series of player portraits with facsimile signatures during the 1948/49 season. A postcard and a photocard featuring the same 11 players were also issued during this period.

Phil Rookes signed from Bradford City in 1938 before serving in the Royal Navy on HMS Argonaut during World War Two. A regular at right-back after the war, he picked up a championship medal in 1949 and played three more games in 1949/50 before signing for Colchester United in 1951. Rookes departed Fratton Park having made a total of 121 appearances.

BARRATT & CO. 1947–50.

Famous Footballers

3 x 50 cards. Unnumbered. D. Reid, J.W. Dickinson. (62 x 44mm).

Barratt & Co. continued their *Famous Footballers* series after the war, issuing three sets of 50 cards between 1947 and 1950. Duggie Reid featured in all three, while Jimmy Dickinson was included in 1949/50. Each of the series can be found with variations in the type of ink and card used. These cards can also be found with the reverse inverted.

Duggie Reid joined Pompey from Stockport County in 1946 and finished his first season as top scorer with 29 goals. Famous for a ferocious shot which earned him the nickname 'Thunderboots', he once broke the net scoring a penalty against Manchester City at Fratton Park. His hat-trick on the final day of the 1949/50 season proved invaluable as Pompey secured the championship on goal average.

When Reid's playing career came to an end he took up the position of head groundsman which he held until 1978, developing the pitch into one of the finest in the country.

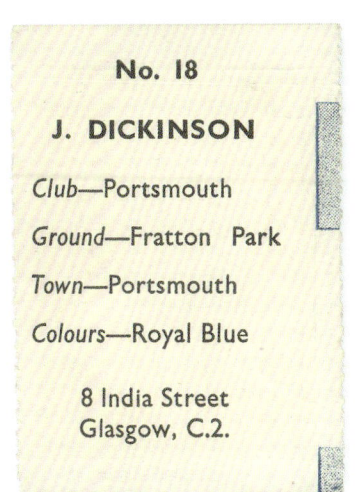

CITY BAKERIES. 1948–54.

Football Shields

300+ cards. Unnumbered. Portsmouth. (82 x 72mm).

Over 300 varieties of *Football Shields* were given away by City Bakeries, a Glaswegian chain of bakeries and tea rooms, with their products during the late 1940s and early 1950s. The series included both generic match-action and player portrait illustrations printed in the colours of the featured club. Two Portsmouth versions are known to exist.

M.M. FRAME. 1948.

Sport Stars

48 cards. No. 18. J. Dickinson. (63 x 42mm).

Issued by M.M. Frame of Glasgow, this series was distributed in booklets of five perforated cards and featured leading football, swimming, boxing, rugby, athletics and cricket stars.

M.M. FRAME. 1950.

Sport Aces

48 cards. No. 38. E.A.E. Butler, No. 45. James Dickinson. (63 x 42mm).

Another collection issued by M.M. Frame, this time documenting footballers, boxers, speedway riders, golfers, cricketers and swimmers. The reverse of each card features a range of historical statistics.

Goalkeeper Ernie Butler signed from Bath City and made his first-team debut in October 1946 versus Sunderland, replacing Harry Walker. He was the only ever-present player during both championship winning seasons and conceded just 80 goals in 84 matches.

A broken wrist sustained in late 1952 kept Butler out for a year and ultimately led to his retirement in 1953 following 222 league appearances for Pompey, his only Football League club. He is shown in action during the 1-1 Charity Shield draw with Wolverhampton Wanderers at Highbury in October 1949.

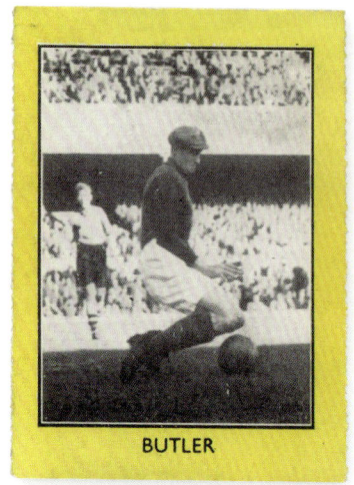

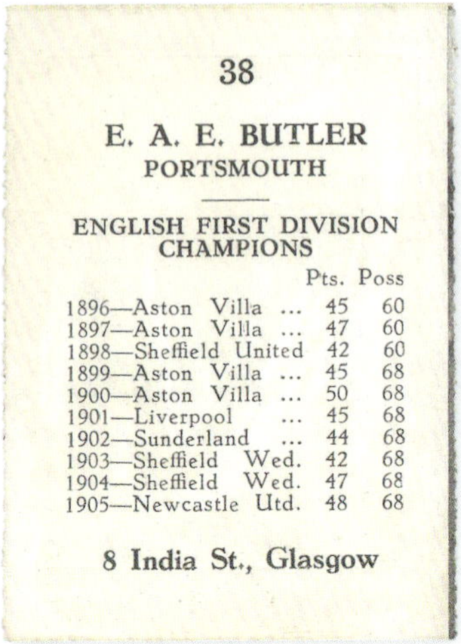

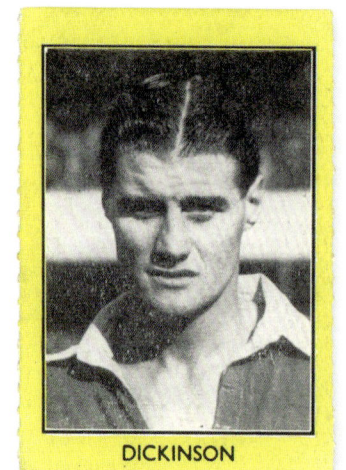

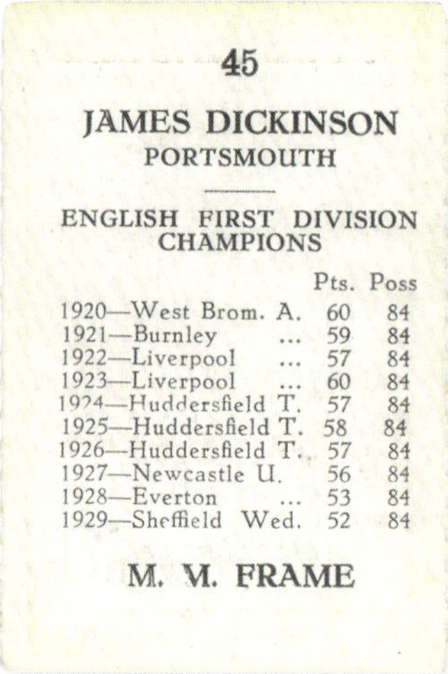

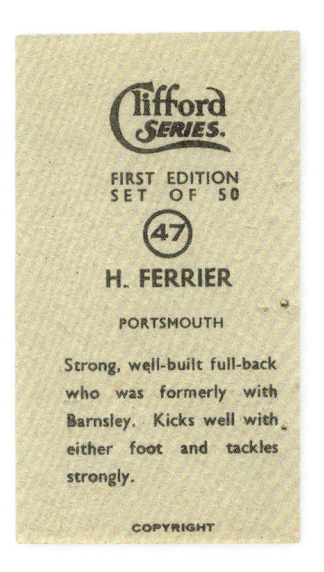

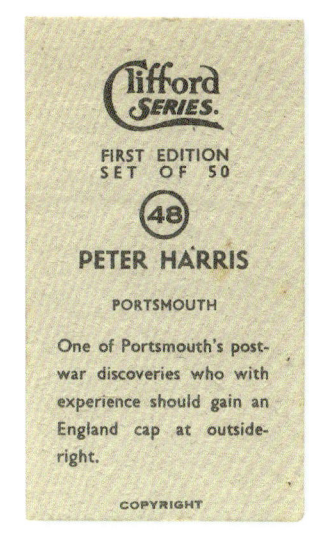

CLIFFORD. 1950.

Clifford Series (First Edition)

50 cards. No. 47. H. Ferrier, No. 48. Peter Harris. (71 x 40mm).

Clifford's black and white series of 50 British football stars was issued in booklets of nine and the cards are usually found with staple holes on the left-hand edge.

Harry Ferrier signed from Barnsley in 1946 having appeared for Pompey as a guest player during World War Two. He was the club's first-choice left-back throughout both championship campaigns and filled in as captain when Reg Flewin was injured. In 1953 he joined Gloucester City as a player-manager following 257 league and cup appearances.

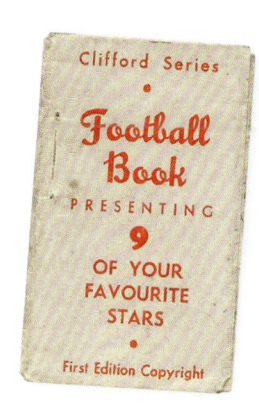

ODHAMS PRESS. 1951.
Sporting Personalities

52 postcards. No. 49. Len Phillips. (138 x 88mm).

Odhams Press, a newspaper and magazine publisher, advertised a series of *Sporting Personalities* postcards in several titles throughout 1951.

Len Phillips, who had taken part in the Normandy D-Day landings on 6th June 1944 with the Royal Marines, was recommended to Pompey by a marine corporal. By 1948 he had established himself in the first-team as a skilful inside-forward and played a pivotal role during the championship seasons.

By the time injury brought Phillips' professional career to an end in 1956 he had made 272 league and cup appearances for Pompey, scoring 54 goals, and been selected to represent England on three occasions. He later played non-league football for Poole Town and Bath City.

LEN PHILLIPS

ADVENTURE/THE ROVER/ THE HOTSPUR/THE WIZARD. 1951.

Famous Footballers

179 paper cut-outs. Unnumbered. J. Dickinson, R. Flewin, J. Froggatt, D. Reid, J. Stephen. (54 x 43mm).

These *Famous Footballers* cut-outs can be found printed in both black and blue ink.

Scotland international full-back Jimmy Stephen began his career with Bradford Park Avenue before joining Pompey in October 1949, making his debut the following month in a 2-2 draw against Sunderland at Fratton Park. He started the following season at right-back and was a regular in the side until 1953/54 when injury restricted him to only five appearances. When released by Pompey in 1955, Stephen joined Yeovil Town.

SPORT. 1949/50.

Team Picture Book

36 cards (six booklets). Unnumbered. Portsmouth F.C. 1949-50. Booklet 3. (100 x 125mm).

36 coloured team photographs issued as six stapled *Team Picture Books* in exchange for coupons which were printed in issues of Sport magazine during the 1949/50 season.

CARRERAS. 1951.

Famous Footballers

50 cards. No. 33. Jack Froggatt, No. 42. Jim Dickinson. (130 x 58mm, 67 x 36mm cut from slide).

Carreras were one of only a few firms to resume cigarette card production after the war. Paper was in short supply so the designs were printed directly on to the slides inside packets of their Turf brand cigarettes. More commonly found cut down, this series was also printed in pairs with packets of 20 cigarettes.

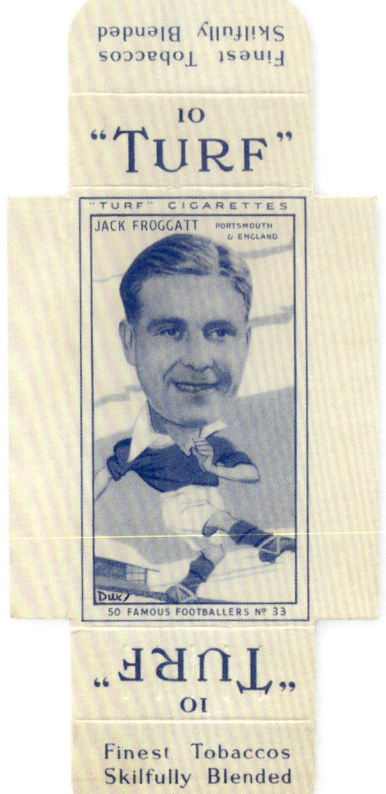

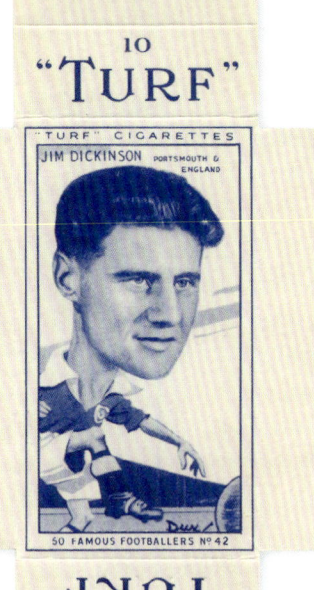

ADVENTURE/THE HOTSPUR/ THE ROVER/THE WIZARD. 1952.

Famous Goal-Getters

24 x 4 paper cut-outs. Unnumbered. Value 10 Goals, Value 20 Goals, Value 30 Goals, Value 50 Goals. D. Reid. (57 x 35mm).

A collection of 96 paper cut-outs which could be saved and sent away for the chance to win a football or a pair of football boots.

PALMER MANN. 1953/54.

Sifta Sam's Series of 24 Famous Footballers

24 cards. No. 6. Jack Froggatt, No. 21. J.W. Dickinson, No. 24. Norman Uprichard. (70 x 32mm).

Palmer Mann's *Famous Footballers* cards were printed on to the outside of boxes of Sifta Sam salt.

Jack Froggatt, who played as an outside-left and centre-half for both Pompey and England, was serving in the RAF when he was offered a trial at the club in 1945. He made 304 league and cup appearances across nine seasons, scoring 72 goals, before transferring to Leicester City in 1954. When he retired from the game, Froggatt returned to Portsmouth to become a publican.

BARRATT & CO. 1950–53.

Famous Footballers (New Series)

3 x 50 cards. No. 16. J. Froggatt, No. 31 and No. 47. J. Dickinson, No. 38. L. Phillips, No. 45. D. Reid, No. 50 J. Scoular. (62 x 44mm).

Barratt & Co.'s *New Series* of *Famous Footballers* was issued across three seasons between 1950 and 1953.

Jimmy Scoular partnered Jimmy Dickinson at right-half and his all-round footballing ability saw him make his name as both a fearsome tackler and an accurate passer of the ball. Having served as a submarine engineer during World War Two, Scoular won two championship medals with Pompey before he was sold to Newcastle United in 1953. He captained his new side to victory in the 1955 FA Cup Final ahead of a successful move into management at Cardiff City.

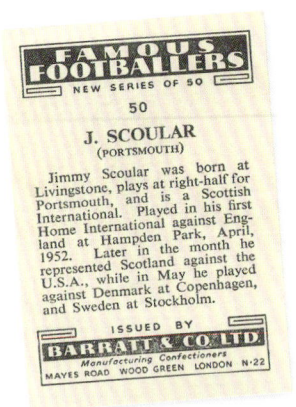

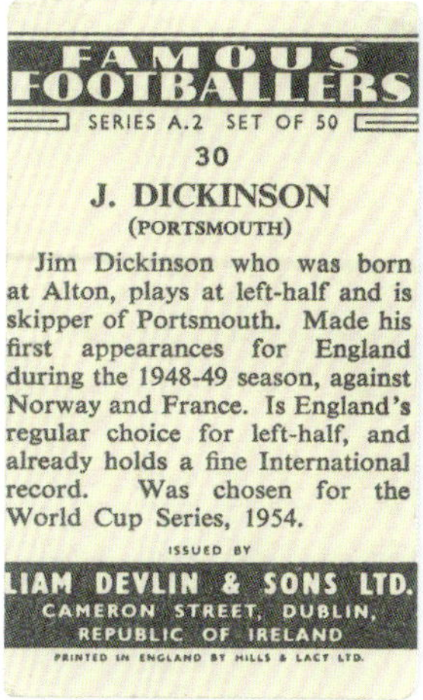

BARRATT & CO. 1953.

Famous Footballers (Series A.1)

50 cards. No. 5. C. Vaughan, No. 7. J. Froggatt, No. 43. J. Dickinson. (62 x 44mm).

Barratt & Co. issued the 'A' series of *Famous Footballers* for 15 years, beginning with *A.1* in 1953 through to *A.15* in 1968.

Centre-forward Charlie Vaughan featured in *Series A.1* along with Jack Froggatt and Jimmy Dickinson. He had been a prolific goalscorer at both Sutton United and Charlton Athletic before transferring to Pompey in 1953. Vaughan scored 16 goals in 29 appearances.

BARRATT & CO. 1954.

Famous Footballers (Series A.2)

50 cards. No. 30. J. Dickinson (front of card shown). (62 x 44mm).

LIAM DEVLIN & SONS. 1954.

Famous Footballers (Series A.2)

50 cards. No. 30. J. Dickinson (back of card shown). (62 x 36mm).

Liam Devlin & Sons of Ireland issued *Famous Footballers* cards, under licence from Barratt & Co., during the early 1950s. Sometimes issued trimmed down in size to fit into smaller packets, the cards were identical to Barratt's apart from the firm's details at the foot of the reverse.

CHIX CONFECTIONERY. 1953.

Famous Footballers (No. 1 Series)

48 cards. No. 3. Jimmy Dickinson, No. 21. Jack Froggatt. (96 x 49mm).

The first half of Chix's *Famous Footballers (No. 1 Series)* features illustrations, with the second half being photographic. Several printings of this series were issued, and variations can be found in the information on the reverse. The cards can be found inscribed set of 24, set of 48 (numbers 1 to 24 only), numbers 1 to 24, numbers 25 to 48 and numbers 1 to 48, and with both Slough and London addresses.

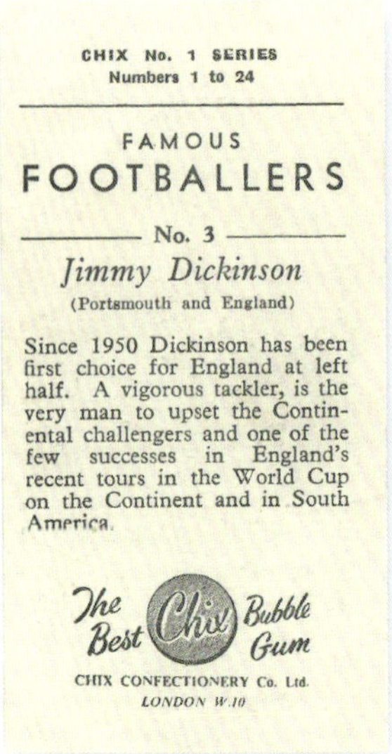

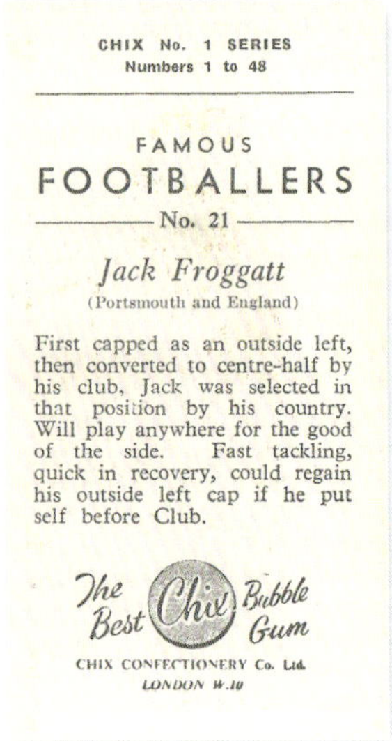

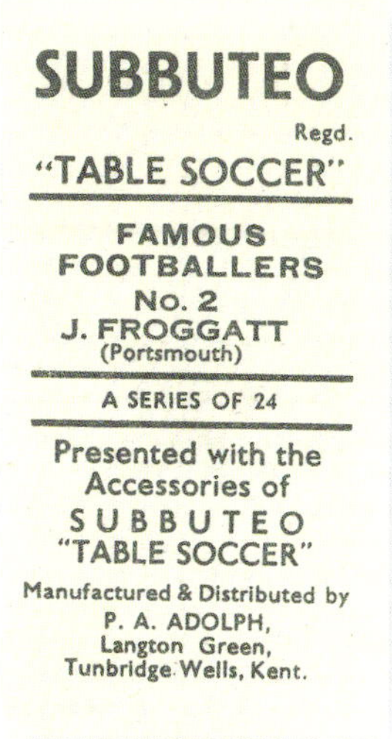

SUNDAY EMPIRE NEWS. 1953.

Famous Footballers of To-Day

48 cards. No. 3. J. Dickinson (spelt incorrectly on card). (75 x 39mm).

Issued in stapled booklets of eight cards, designed to be trimmed across the top and mounted in an album.

A&BC CHEWING GUM. 1954.

"All Sport" Series

120 cards (36 footballers). No. 14. Jimmy Dickinson. (75 x 45mm).

Between 1953 and 1974 A&BC issued dozens of sets covering a wide variety of subjects. The *"All Sport" Series* was A&BC's first to include footballers.

P.A. ADOLPH (SUBBUTEO). 1954.

Famous Footballers (First Series)

24 cards. No. 2. J. Froggatt. (66 x 35mm).

A series of 50 larger photographic cards, comprising the two series of 24, plus two additional cards, was also issued during the same year.

DAILY HERALD. 1951–54.

Soccer Stars

32 cards. No. 5. Reg Flewin, No. 27. Ike Clarke. (61 x 38mm).

Daily Herald's series of *Soccer Stars* can be found both with and without 'SPORTFOTO' inscribed at the foot of the cards. Centre-forward Ike Clarke starred in the championship-winning sides, finishing the 1949/50 season as top goalscorer with 17 goals.

CADET SWEETS. 1953.

Footballers

50 transfers. Image shown flipped as issued. No. 38. Jackie Henderson. (67 x 35mm).

CADET SWEETS. 1957.

Footballers

50 cards. No. 16. Norman Uprichard (Portsmouth and Eire). (65 x 35mm).

Goalkeeper Norman Uprichard signed from Swindon Town in 1952, taking the place of Ernie Butler. A Northern Ireland international, he played in the 1958 World Cup Finals in Sweden as his country reached the quarter-finals. Uprichard made almost 200 appearances during a seven-season stay at Fratton Park before signing for Southend United. A plain-back version of this series was issued the same year by Gee Products.

THE ROVER. 1953–56.

Famous Footballers

1,013 paper cut-outs (including those issued 1968–70). Unnumbered. P. Harris, J. Henderson, C. Rutter, C. Vaughan, J. Froggatt, R. Flewin, P. Neil, J. Mansell, J. Dickinson. (65 x 45mm).

Famous Footballers were printed on the front covers of The Rover comic between 1953 and 1956, then again between 1968 and 1970, collectively totalling 1,013 portraits.

Cyril Rutter was a dockyard apprentice when he signed for Pompey in 1951. The centre-half made 185 league and cup appearances between 1953 and 1963, experiencing two relegations, before picking up a Third Division championship medal in 1961/62.

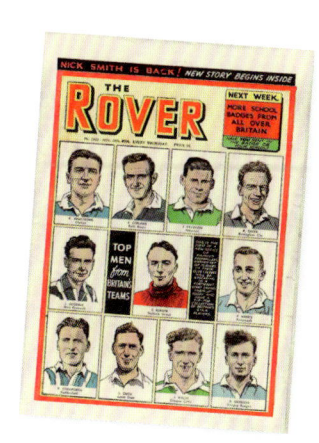

HOBBIES LTD. 1954.

Famous Footballers

8 paper cut-outs. Unnumbered. Jack Froggatt. (76 x 65mm).

One of a sheet of eight footballers issued with the Hobbies 1954 Handbook. These were intended to be stuck down to plywood and cut out using a fret saw.

A. & J. DONALDSON. 1955.

Gold Cup Football Teams

145 known cards. Unnumbered. Portsmouth. (76 x 55mm).

This series is believed to have been issued to commemorate the inauguration of the European Cup competition.

BARRATT & CO. 1956 AND 1957.

Famous Footballers – Series A.4 (1956) and Series A.5. (1957)

60 cards. Series A.4. No. 9. Series A.5. No. 39. P. Harris. (65 x 35mm).

Peter Harris appeared in both *Series A.4* and *Series A.5* featuring identical artwork on the front of the card. *Series A.4* marked a departure from the familiar *Famous Footballers* card dimensions to a cigarette card-size format.

NEWS CHRONICLE. 1955/56.
Pocket Portraits

803 cards. Unnumbered.
J. Dickinson, J. Gordon, P. Gunter,
P. Harris, J. Henderson, J. McGhee,
J. Mansell, P. Neil, R. Pickett, D. Rees,
J. Reid, N. Uprichard. (86 x 62mm).

The News Chronicle's series of over 800 black and white *Pocket Portrait* cards featured twelve Pompey players, including Johnny Gordon and Jack Mansell.

Portsmouth-born inside-forward and right-half Johnny Gordon had two spells with the club between 1951 and 1967, scoring 116 goals in 486 league and cup appearances. During a successful three-season spell with Birmingham City between 1958 and 1961 he was the leading scorer in 1959/60, and played in both legs of the 1960 Inter-Cities Fairs Cup Final against Barcelona.

Left-back Jack Mansell signed from Cardiff City in 1953 and represented Pompey for five years. He was ever-present during the 1954/55 season as Pompey recorded a third-place finish in the First Division. When appendicitis ended his playing career prematurely at the age of 30, Mansell moved into management at both Rotherham United and Reading.

THE WIZARD. 1955.

Famous Footballers

25 cards. No. 21. Jackie Henderson. (68 x 36mm).

Sheets of cards were regularly given away across a range of D.C. Thomson's publications. Jackie Henderson featured in the *Famous Footballers* series, issued with The Wizard in 1955.

Henderson signed for Pompey as a 17 year old and was utilised both as a centre-forward and an outside-left, scoring 73 goals in 230 league and cup appearances. A move to Wolverhampton Wanderers in 1958 was followed by a switch to Arsenal the following year, before he saw out his playing days at Fulham.

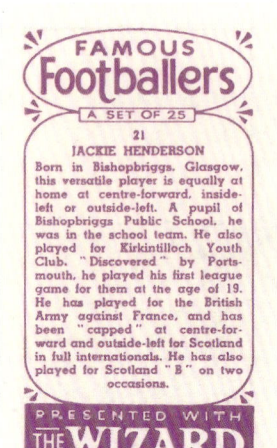

THE WIZARD. 1956.

Famous Footballers

24 cards. No. 12. Jimmy Dickinson. (68 x 36mm).

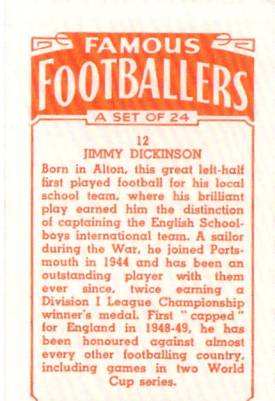

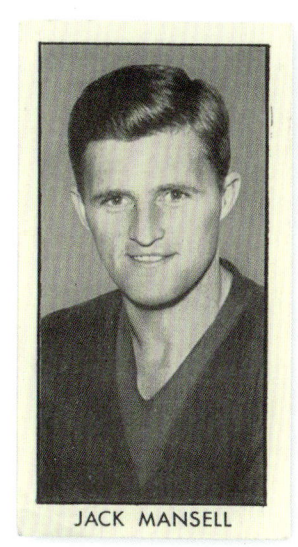

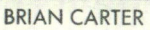

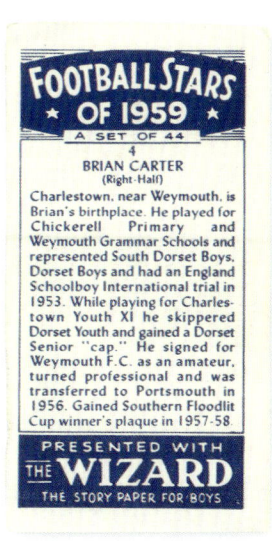

ADVENTURE. 1957.
Football Stars

48 cards. No. 7. Jack Mansell. (68 x 36mm).

THE WIZARD. 1959.
Football Stars of 1959

44 cards. No. 4. Brian Carter. (68 x 36mm).

Signed from non-league Weymouth in 1956, half-back Brian Carter made his Pompey debut in April 1958. He joined Bristol Rovers in the summer of 1961 having made 51 league and cup appearances.

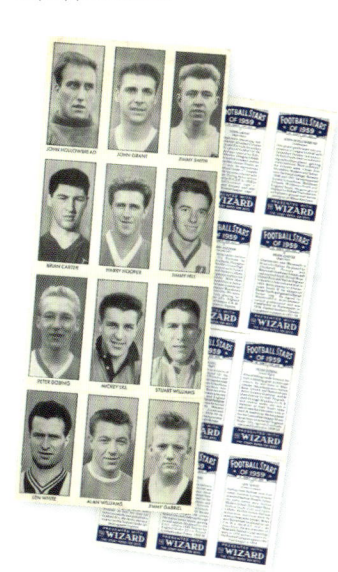

DAILY EXPRESS. 1956/57.
Football Teams

50 known cards. Unnumbered.
Portsmouth F.C. 1956–57. (88 x 140mm).

COLINVILLE. 1958.
British International Football Stars

48 cards. Unnumbered.
Norman Uprichard. (29 x 22mm).

ADVENTURE. 1959.
World Footballers of Tomorrow

42 stickers. Unnumbered.
Derek Dougan. (70 x 43mm).

Centre-forward Derek Dougan joined from Belfast Distillery in 1957, making his Pompey debut at Old Trafford during a 3-0 victory versus Manchester United. He earned his first Northern Ireland cap at the 1958 World Cup Finals, alongside Pompey goalkeeper Norman Uprichard. Dougan was sold to Blackburn Rovers in March 1959 having scored nine goals in 36 league and cup appearances.

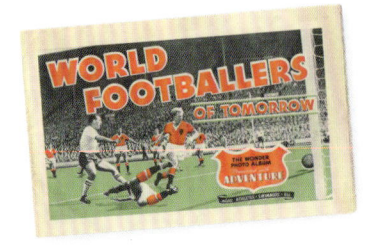

PORTSMOUTH F.C. 1958-59

Left to right (Back row) P. Gunter, J. Phillips, N. Uprichard, B. Hayward, J. Dickinson, T. Casey; (Front row) P. Harris, J. Gordon (now with Birmingham City), R. Saunders, D. Harris, R. Newman

Series A   No. 1

Arsenal v. Portsmouth 4—0 in London.

Strong of Portsmouth makes a good opening.

TIP TOP
Sales Company Valletta-Malta

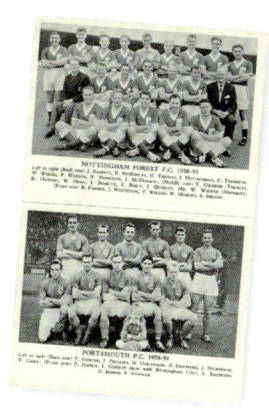

TIGER. 1958/59.

Football Teams

28 cards. Unnumbered. Portsmouth F.C. 1958–59. (95 x 112mm).

Printed in pairs or groups of four, these are usually found cut down to individual cards. Originally issued as a pair with Nottingham Forest.

TIP TOP SALES COMPANY. 1958.

European Football Action (Series A)

25 cards. No. 1. Arsenal v Portsmouth 4-0 in London. (73 x 44mm).

Maltese firm Tip Top Sales Company issued a retrospective series of 25 *European Football Action* cards in 1958. George Strong is pictured punching the ball clear during the 4-0 defeat away to Arsenal in April 1937.

1940–1959 | 107

LAMBERTS OF NORWICH. 1958.
Football Clubs and Badges

25 cards. No. 19. Portsmouth.
(65 x 35mm).

Tea company Lamberts of Norwich issued the colourful *Football Clubs and Badges* series in 1958. Identical sets were also given away by several other firms, including Johnny Bunny Medicines and Amalgamated Tobacco Corp. Ltd.

SWEETULE PRODUCTS. 1959.
Football Club Nicknames

25 cards. No. 10. Portsmouth.
(65 x 35mm).

Sweetule Products' series of 25 *Football Club Nicknames* cards gave clues to the identity of the club featured, with the answer revealed on the reverse.

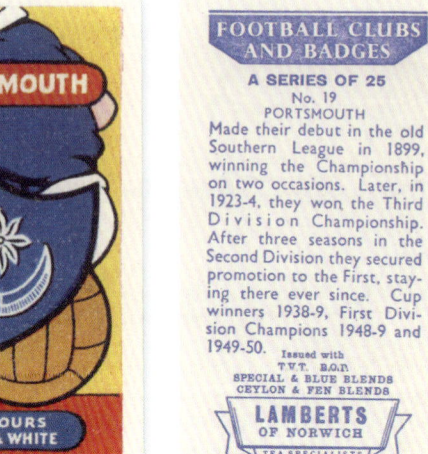

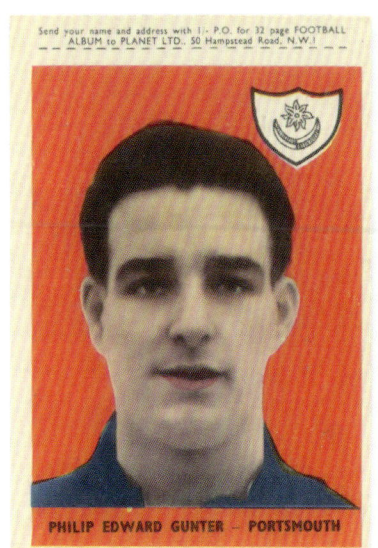

A&BC CHEWING GUM. 1958/59.

Topstars Famous Footballers (Series 2)

92 cards (Series 1 and 2). No. 60. James Dickinson. No. 67. Philip Edward Gunter. (95 x 64mm).

Topstars Famous Footballers, A&BC's first football-specific series, was issued during the 1958/59 season.

Portsmouth-born Phil Gunter signed in 1949 aged 17, making his debut versus Newcastle in October 1951. He made 357 appearances during his 15 years at Fratton Park before transferring to Aldershot. A deeply religious man, Gunter was excused from playing matches on Good Friday and Christmas Day.

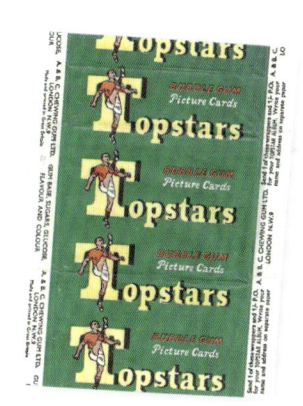

1940–1959 | 109

A&BC CHEWING GUM. 1958.

Footballer (Football Quiz)

98 cards. No. 88. Phil Gunter. (95 x 67mm).

SOIREE CIGARETTES. 1958/59.

Famous Footballers

48 cards. No. 43. Jimmy Dickinson (spelt incorrectly on card). (60 x 42mm).

An exceptionally scarce series of cards, issued only in Mauritius, printed on the slides inside packets of Soiree Filter Tipped cigarettes.

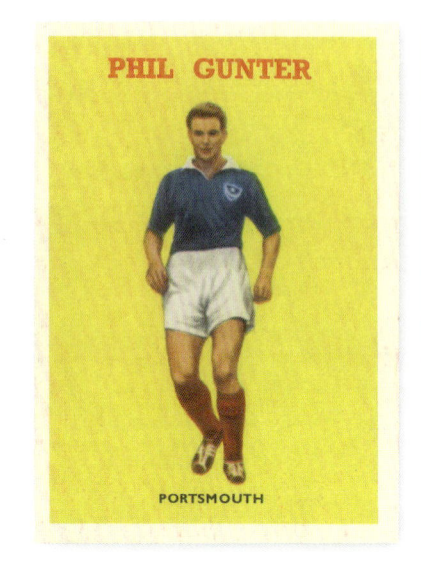

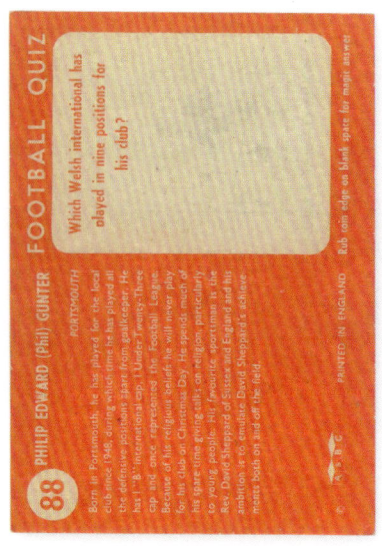

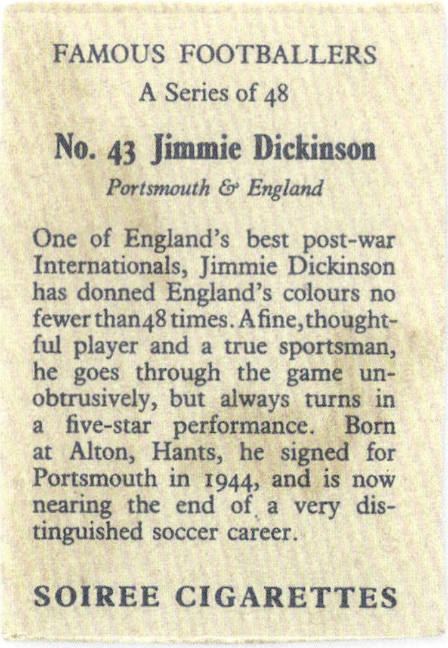

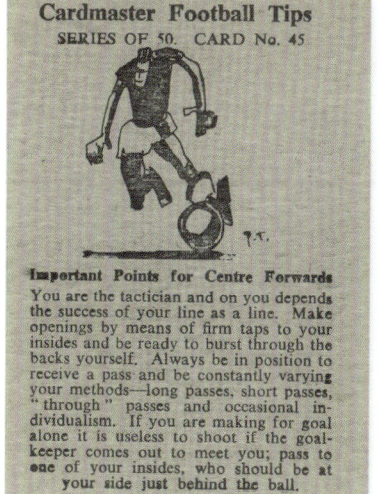

THE MASTER VENDING COMPANY. 1958.

Cardmaster Football Tips

50 cards. Two varieties. No. 25 and No. 29. Jimmy Dickinson (spelt incorrectly on card), No. 43 and No. 45. Peter Harris. (95 x 67mm).

The Master Vending Company issued just eight series in the late 1950s before vanishing from the gum card scene. The 1958 series of *Cardmaster Football Tips* can be found with brown, cream and grey coloured backs. Illustrated by the globally acclaimed sports artist Paul Trevillion, the 'Master of Movement' also drew the artwork for the *Did You Know* series the following year.

Portsmouth-born outside-right Peter Harris, Pompey's all-time top goalscorer, was spotted playing for Gosport Borough and made enough of an impression during wartime matches to sign for the club he watched from the terraces. He was a regular during the title-winning seasons, hitting 17, then 16 goals. He won two England caps and would undoubtedly have made more appearances for the national side but for the form of Stanley Matthews and Tom Finney. Harris scored a total of 209 goals in 514 league and cup games during his 14 years with Pompey.

THE MASTER VENDING COMPANY. 1959.

Did You Know

50 cards. No. 13. Basil Hayward, No. 14. Ron Saunders, No. 25. Harry Harris, No. 33. Tommy McGhee, No. 50. Jimmy Dickinson. (95 x 67mm).

A year after their *Cardmaster Football Tips* collection, The Master Vending Company released the *Did You Know* series. Variations can be found with both light and dark blue backgrounds, and cream and grey coloured backs.

Basil Hayward joined from Third Division Port Vale and endured a tough time at centre-half during the 1958/59 season as Pompey were relegated to the Second Division with the Football League's worst defensive record. Hayward made 16 appearances the following season, including 12 as a centre-forward which brought a return of four goals. He was released in 1960 having made 49 league and cup appearances and was appointed player-manager at Yeovil Town.

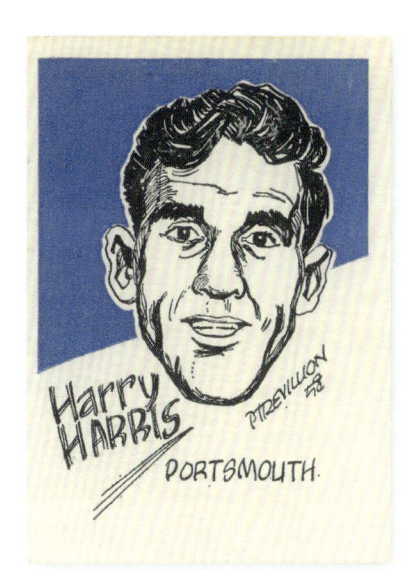

Harry Harris joined Pompey from Newport County and made over 400 appearances between 1958 and 1971, scoring 49 goals. He started life at Fratton Park as a striker but was later also utilised as a midfielder and central-defender. He re-joined the Welsh club on loan in 1970, but returned as captain for what was a farewell appearance in the final game of the 1970/71 season against Leicester City.

Tommy McGhee served as a Petty Officer in the Royal Navy and was an amateur footballer with Wealdstone when he signed for First Division Pompey in May 1954. He made his debut during a 5-0 home win over Everton the following November and proved to be a valuable member of the side which finished the season in third place. McGhee left for Reading in 1959, the year Pompey were relegated to the Second Division.

SECOND DIVISION CONSOLIDATION

The drop down to the Second Division in 1959 was the first relegation experienced by the club since joining the Football League in 1920. Pompey failed to adjust to life in the second tier and narrowly avoided consecutive relegations by just two points before the 1960/61 season saw matters go from bad to worse. A financial crisis enveloped the club as the team continued to struggle and manager Freddie Cox was dismissed in February 1961. His replacement George Smith was unable to halt the downturn in form and his side, primarily made up of young and inexperienced players, suffered a second relegation in the space of three years.

Smith's appointment soon proved to be a shrewd one, however, as the 1961/62 season began with a 12-match unbeaten run. Pompey were top of Division Three at Christmas and by Easter the championship had been won, aided by 26 goals from the prolific Ron Saunders. Promotion brought a renewed sense of optimism, but Pompey failed to progress. Saunders was sold on the eve of the 1964/65 season and without his regular haul of goals another relegation battle ensued. A dramatic equaliser in the dying minutes of the final game of the season away to Northampton Town, which salvaged a 1-1 draw, ultimately preserved Pompey's Second Division status.

A succession of mid-to-lower table finishes during the second half of the decade was interrupted by a brief push for promotion in 1967/68. Pompey sat top of the table in September, but their form stuttered after Christmas. Club-record signing Mike Trebilcock, Everton's 1966 FA Cup Final goalscoring hero, arrived in February 1968 but with only one goal in 13 league appearances, he failed to provide the firepower to push the team up the table. His form mirrored that of the side as a whole, and just three wins from the last 13 matches resulted in a fifth-place finish. It was the closest Pompey would come to reaching the top division for almost twenty years.

1960–1969

DICKSON ORDE & CO. 1960.

Footballers

50 cards. No. 35. Jim Dickinson. (62 x 35mm).

ANGLO-AMERICAN CHEWING GUM. 1960.

Famous Soccer Clubs (Series 1)

112 wax wrappers. No. 57. Portsmouth. (67 x 46mm).

In addition to cards, gum manufacturers produced sets that were printed on to the wax wrappers their products were packaged in. Anglo-American Chewing Gum's *Famous Soccer Clubs* series was issued with their 'Bell Boy' brand.

ROVER AND ADVENTURE. 1961.

ABC Chart of Football Colours

130 paper cut-outs. No. 89. P. Gunter. (34 x 31mm).

An update to the *ABC Chart of Football Colours*, this time featuring Phil Gunter, was issued 30 years after the original.

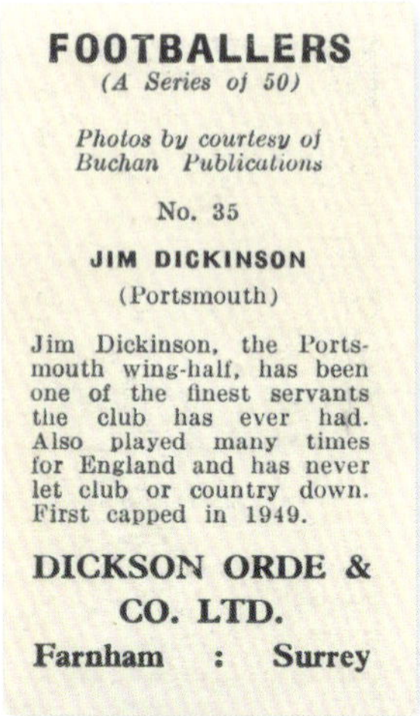

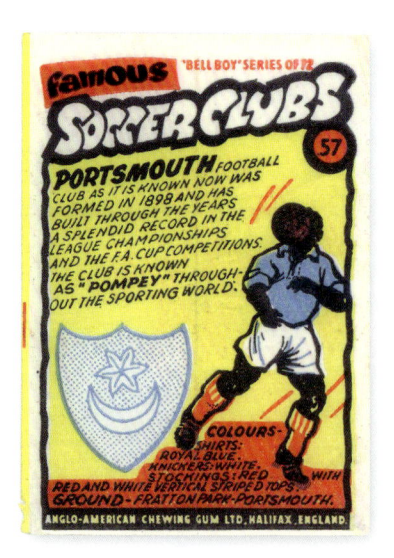

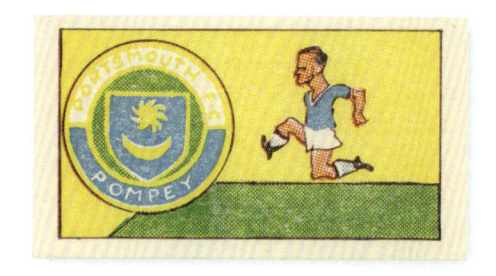

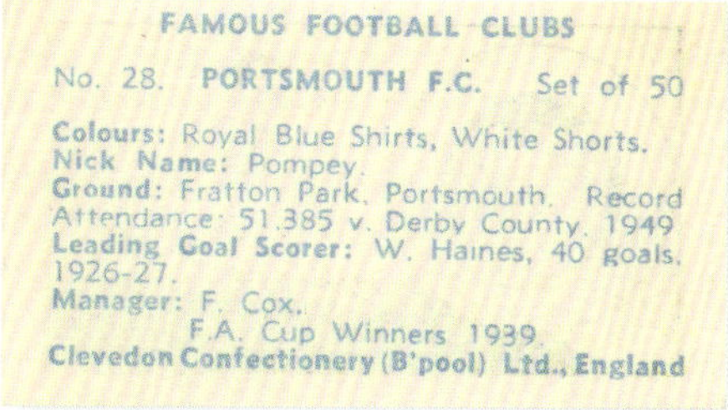

CLEVEDON CONFECTIONERY. 1961.
Famous Football Clubs

50 cards. No. 28. Portsmouth F.C.
(32 x 57mm).

CLEVEDON CONFECTIONERY. 1961.
Famous Footballers

50 cards. No. 24. Peter Harris.
(56 x 33mm).

Pompey were represented in both the *Famous Football Clubs* and *Famous Footballers* series, issued by Clevedon Confectionery in 1961.

The *Famous Footballers* series was illustrated by Stan Jones of Crosby, Merseyside, who owned a tobacconist which stocked Clevedon Confectionery products. He offered to draw a set of footballers for the firm that was subsequently issued with packets of sweet cigarettes.

CHIX CONFECTIONERY. 1961.

Famous Footballers

50 cards. No. 9. Alex Wilson. (95 x 67mm).

Scotland full-back Alex Wilson served Pompey for 18 years between 1949 and 1967. On the last day of the 1964/65 season away to Northampton Town, in what was to be Jimmy Dickinson's final appearance, he scored one of the most important goals in the club's history. Trailing 1-0 and with Pompey needing a single point to avoid relegation to the Third Division, Wilson equalised with just five minutes remaining.

A&BC CHEWING GUM. 1961.

Footballers

64 cards. No. 30. Allan Brown, No. 55. Johnny Gordon. (89 x 63mm).

Inside-forward Allan Brown made his Pompey debut alongside Johnny Gordon, who had rejoined from Birmingham City, towards the end of the 1960/61 season. They could not help prevent the club dropping into the Third Division but were both important members of the side which won the championship the following season. A Scotland international, Brown made 14 appearances for his country between 1950 and 1954, scoring six goals.

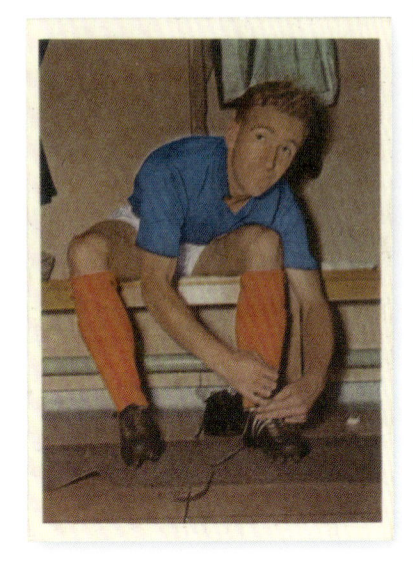

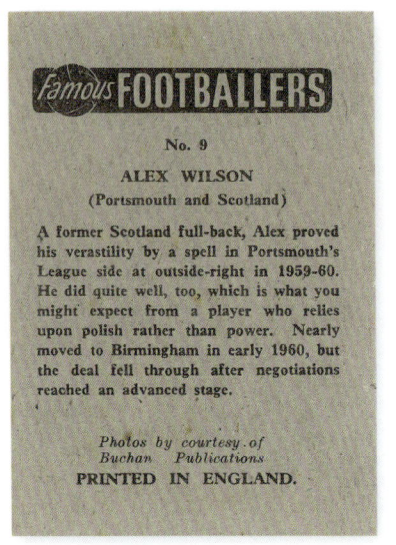

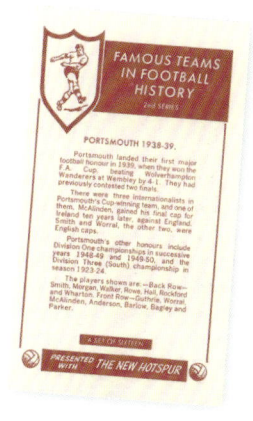

THE NEW HOTSPUR. 1962.

Famous Teams in Football History (2nd Series)

16 cards. Unnumbered. Portsmouth 1939. (78 x 140mm).

A retrospective series featuring Pompey's victorious 1939 FA Cup Final squad.

PEPYS. 1964.

"GOAL!" The Soccer Card Game (Second Edition)

44 cards. Unnumbered. Portsmouth. (87 x 57mm).

Produced by Pepys, the firm that issued *It's a Goal!* in 1939. *"Goal!" The Soccer Card Game* consisted of 44 cards, featuring clubs from the top two divisions. The first edition was issued in 1959 and can be identified by the reverse, which shows the ball in the bottom left-hand corner.

A&BC CHEWING GUM. 1963.

Footballer (Make-a-Photo)

110 cards (Series 1 and 2). No. 32. John Gordon, No. 92. Ron Saunders, No. 99. Brian Snowdon. (81 x 56mm).

Centre-half Brian Snowdon signed from Blackpool for a fee of £10,000 in 1959, taking over the captaincy from Jimmy Dickinson. He made 43 appearances during the Third Division championship-winning campaign of 1961/62 and was a regular the following season. Snowdon fell out of favour during the early part of the 1963/64 season before transferring to Millwall.

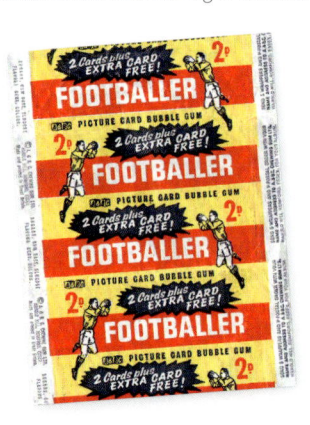

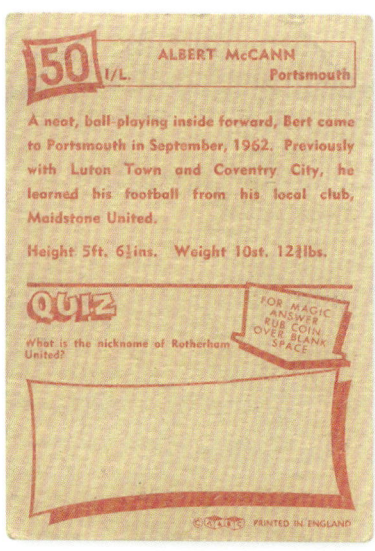

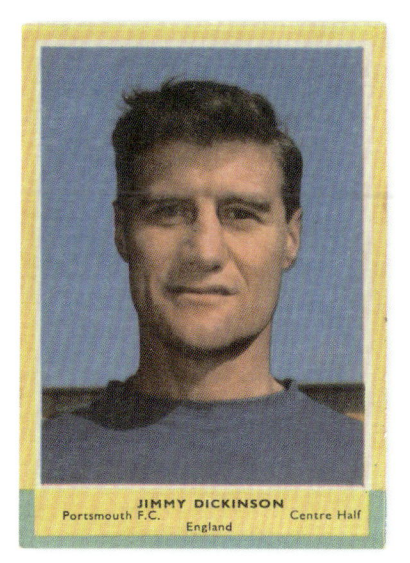

A&BC CHEWING GUM. 1964/65.

Footballer (Quiz)

149 cards. (Series 1, 2 and 3). No. 50. Albert McCann, No. 139. Jimmy Dickinson, No. 146. Ron Saunders. (81 x 56mm).

Albert McCann featured both as a midfielder and as a striker during his 12 years with Pompey, making a total of 397 appearances and scoring 98 goals between 1962 and 1974. An £8,000 signing from Coventry, he soon became a crowd favourite who was known for his hard-working displays and bow-legged gait. On retirement he owned a newsagent's on Winter Road and ran a care home on Hayling Island.

Centre-forward Ron Saunders arrived during the 1958/59 season and was to become the third most potent striker in Pompey's history, behind only John Weddle and Peter Harris in the club's league goalscoring charts. During his first season at Fratton Park he scored 21 goals in 36 league appearances as the club was relegated to the Second Division. He was the leading goalscorer for six consecutive seasons, including an impressive 34 goals in 46 league and cup games in 1963/64, before he was surprisingly sold to Watford for £15,000 the following August. A successful move into management saw him lead Aston Villa to the First Division title in 1981.

DAILY EXPRESS. 1965/66.
Football Teams

13 known cards. Unnumbered. Portsmouth F.C. (85 x 140mm).

A series of black and white postcard-size team groups, issued by the Daily Express during the 1965/66 season.

A&BC CHEWING GUM. 1966/67.
Footballer (Series 2)

110 cards. No. 196. Albert McCann. (55 x 40mm).

Originally printed as a pair, Pompey's Albert McCann was issued alongside Ipswich Town's Cyril Lea.

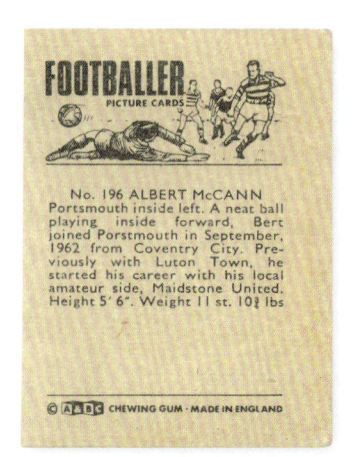

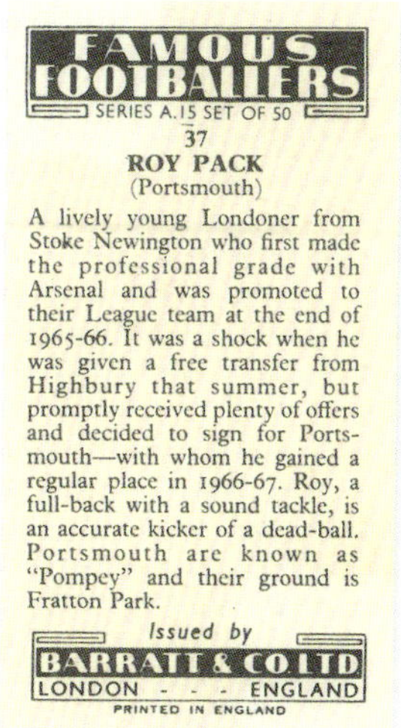

WEBCOSA. 1963–68.
Football Bingo

72+ wax wrappers. Unnumbered. J. McClelland. (64 x 48mm).

Issued with *Football Bingo* gum during the 1960s, these caricatures could be collected and sent away in exchange for a prize. An outside-right, John McClelland made 150 appearances in six seasons with Pompey, scoring 38 goals.

LION AND CHAMPION. 1967.
Lion and Champion Album of Soccer Stars

110 stickers. No. 36. Ray Pointer. (25 x 25mm).

TIGER AND HURRICANE. 1967.
Roy Race's Album of Football Club Badges

110 stickers. No. 77. Portsmouth. (30 x 25mm).

BARRATT & CO. 1967/68.
Famous Footballers (Series A.15)

50 cards. No. 37. Roy Pack. (65 x 35mm).

Barratt's final series of *Famous Footballers* cards featured right-back Roy Pack who signed on a free transfer from Arsenal in 1966 and went on to make 105 league and cup appearances, scoring one goal.

A&BC CHEWING GUM. 1968/69.

Footballer (Series 2)

20 cards. Unnumbered. Portsmouth. (50 x 68mm).

A subset of 20 foil football club emblems, issued with packets of *Footballer (Series 2)* cards.

ANGLO CONFECTIONERY. 1969/70.

Football Stars

84 cards. No. 57. George Ley. (75 x 55mm).

Left-back George Ley spent five years at Fratton Park between 1967 and 1972, playing over 200 league and cup games, before moving to Brighton & Hove Albion, then later to North American Soccer League side Dallas Tornado. In 1968 he beat George Best to the title of best-looking footballer in the country in a competition run by Football League Review magazine.

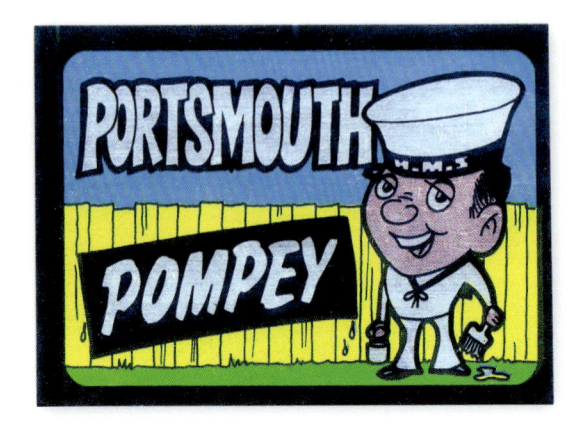

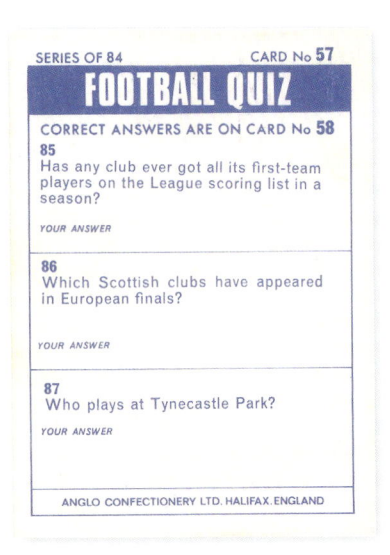

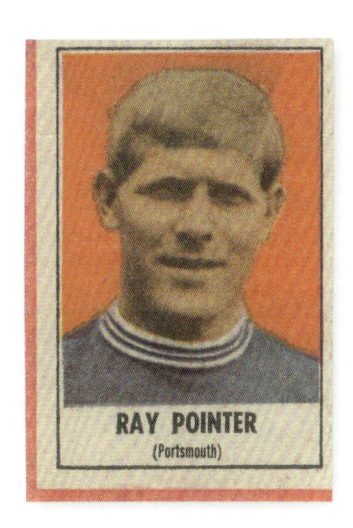

ROVER AND WIZARD. 1968–70.

Famous Footballers

1,013 paper cut-outs (including those issued 1953–56). Unnumbered. Mike Trebilcock, Ray Pointer, George Ley, Norman Piper. (66 x 44mm).

Between August 1968 and October 1970, The Rover revisited its front cover *Famous Footballers* portraits concept of the mid-1950s.

Striker Mike Trebilcock arrived at Pompey for a record £40,000 fee from Everton in January 1968. He scored a memorable last-minute equaliser against Arsenal in the FA Cup Fourth Round tie at Fratton Park in 1971.

Centre-forward Ray Pointer made his name at Burnley, scoring 19 goals in 42 league appearances during the championship-winning season of 1959/60. His goalscoring exploits continued at Bury and Coventry City before he secured a move to Second Division Pompey in 1967.

MAY PORTUGUESA. 1969/70.

Futebol Emblemas, Equipamentos e Bandeiras

180 wrappers. No. 104. Portsmouth Football Club. (110 x 58mm).

Portuguese chewing gum manufacturer May included several British football clubs in this collection of wrappers, issued throughout the 1969/70 season.

1960–1969 | 125

FREEFALL

Following a disappointing 1969/70 season, George Smith's tenure as manager came to an end, with Ron Tindall taking his place. In 1973 John Deacon, who had joined the Pompey board a year earlier, became chairman. He soon replaced Tindall with John Mortimore and as the 1973/74 season approached, several high-profile players on large salaries were brought in as a side supposed to be capable of challenging for promotion was assembled. A 15th-place finish put paid to Deacon's ambitions and a dreadful start to the following campaign, with only one win from the first six matches, cost Mortimore his job.

Next in line to try and turn around Pompey's fortunes was former Liverpool striker Ian St John. After struggling initially, St John's side improved during the latter stages of the season and avoided relegation. The 1975/76 season, however, was a disaster. Just four home wins, the first arriving in January, set the tone and it was no surprise when the team finished bottom of the table and were relegated to the Third Division. Off the pitch, financial problems which had been building for months finally came to a head at the start of the 1976/77 season. The club's top earners were sold and St John was forced to field several youngsters. Inevitably the team struggled and with just three matches remaining St John was suspended leaving Jimmy Dickinson, at the time serving as club secretary, to take charge. Requiring two points to avoid the drop into the basement, a draw at Preston North End, followed by a 3-1 win at home to York City, ensured Pompey escaped at Reading's expense.

Dickinson's first full season in charge ended with Pompey experiencing relegation to the Fourth Division for the first time. For long spells during the 1978/79 season it looked as though Pompey would bounce straight back up but they slipped out of the running, finishing in seventh place. Dickinson suffered a heart attack following a 1-1 draw at Barnsley in March 1979 leaving coach Frank Burrows to take charge until the end of the season.

1970–1979

Two series of *My Favourite Soccer Stars* were produced in the early 1970s. The blue back series was issued in February 1970 across five different comics as perforated sheets of eight cards.

The popularity of the collection led to a second series, this time with red backs, being released in 1971.

BUSTER/LION/SCORCHER/ SMASH/TIGER. 1970.

My Favourite Soccer Stars (blue backs)

160 cards. No. 22. H. Harris (Scorcher). (63 x 45mm).

BUSTER AND JET/LION AND THUNDER/SCORCHER AND SCORE/ TIGER/VALIANT AND TV21. 1971.

My Favourite Soccer Stars (red backs)

160 cards. No. 4. G. Ley (Scorcher and Score), No. 10. R. Pointer (Buster and Jet), No. 13. N. Piper (Scorcher and Score), No. 14. B. Bromley (Tiger), No. 22. N. Jennings (Lion and Thunder). (63 x 45mm).

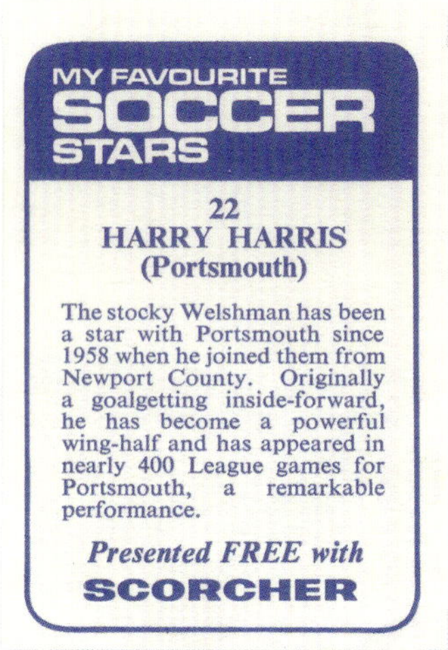

N. Piper *(Portsmouth)*

B. Bromley *(Portsmouth)*

N. Jennings *(Portsmouth)*

MY FAVOURITE SOCCER STARS

22
NICK JENNINGS
(Portsmouth)

A nippy little winger who was born in Somerset and played in local football before joining Plymouth Argyle in 1963. He signed for Portsmouth in January 1967 and has now made 150 first team appearances. Popular with Pompey fans, he is 25 years of age.

Presented FREE with **LION** and **THUNDER**

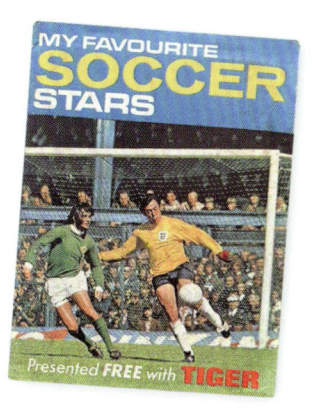

Norman Piper signed from Plymouth Argyle in 1970 for a club record-equalling £50,000. The midfielder played 356 league and cup matches, scoring 57 goals. A fan-favourite, Piper made up for his lack of height with energy and creativity. He left Pompey for Florida in 1978, joining Fort Lauderdale Strikers of the North American Soccer League.

Brian Bromley arrived in 1968 from Bolton Wanderers, where he began his career, for £25,000. The versatile midfielder and forward stayed with Pompey for four years before a move to Brighton & Hove Albion in 1972, then on to Reading the following year.

FKS PUBLISHERS. 1970/71.

Soccer Stars Gala Collection

420 stickers. No. 361. Harry Harris, No. 362. Nicky Jennings. (71 x 48mm). Favourite Second Division Team sheet.

FKS began issuing *The Wonderful World of Soccer Stars* 'picture stamp' albums in the late 1960s, marketing them as 'the new swapping and collecting game'. These collections pre-dated stickers with peelable backs with the pictures needing to be glued into place. *Favourite Second Division Team* sheets featuring 15 players were also available to purchase which could be inserted on page 33 of the *Soccer Stars Gala Collection* album.

Nicky Jennings joined Pompey from Plymouth Argyle in January 1967. A consistent performer, the left-winger's energetic displays were rewarded with the Player of the Year trophy in 1970. Jennings transferred to Exeter City in 1974 having made 227 appearances, with a return of 50 goals.

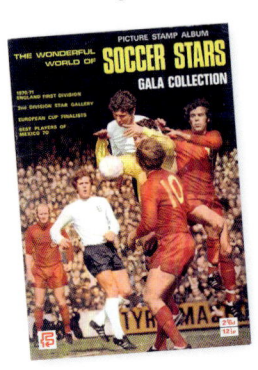

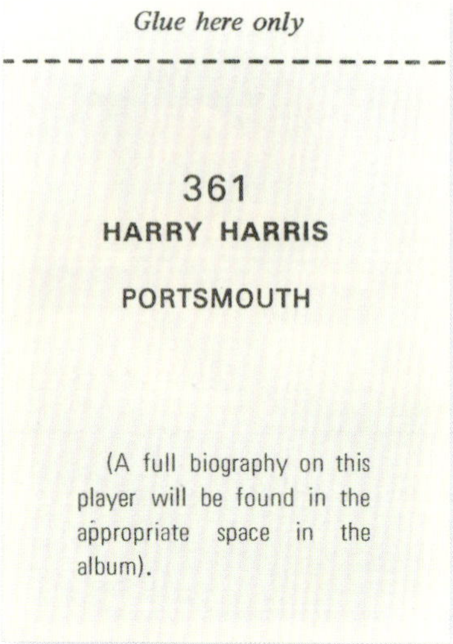

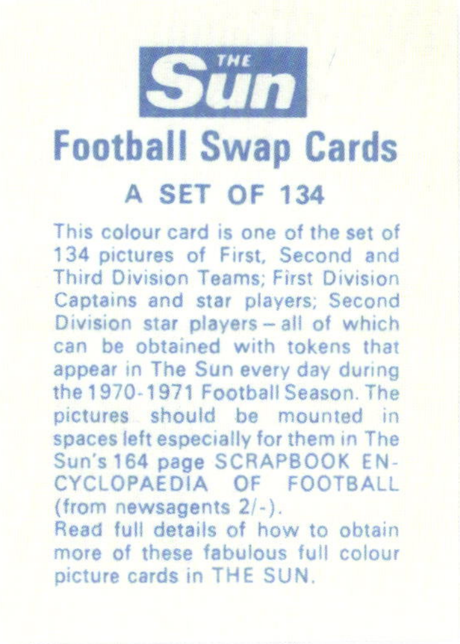

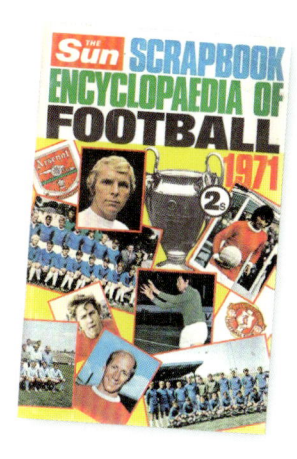

THE SUN. 1970/71.

Football Swap Cards

134 cards. No. 38. Portsmouth (50 x 69mm), No. 128. Norman Piper. (69 x 50mm).

The Sun released the *Football Swap Cards* series in 1970/71. Tokens printed in the newspaper each day could be sent away in return for a selection of cards. The set included the teams of the First, Second and Third Divisions, plus First Division Captains and Star Players, and Second Division Star Players. The *Scrapbook Encyclopaedia of Football 1971* album was issued to house the collection. Pompey were represented on two cards, a team photograph with a squad listing on the reverse, and club captain Norman Piper.

DAILY MIRROR. 1971.
Mirrorcard – Star Soccer Sides

100 cards. No. 38. Portsmouth.
(44 x 76mm).

The Daily Mirror's *Mirrorcard – Star Soccer Sides* cards were issued in exchange for coupons printed in the newspaper. The cards were intended to be slotted into the accompanying *Bobby Moore Gallery of Soccer Sides* wall chart.

DAILY MIRROR. 1971.
My Club

100 cards. Unnumbered. Portsmouth.
(100 x 150mm).

Once all the *Star Soccer Sides* cards had been collected, a larger *My Club* card could be purchased to personalise and complete the wall chart.

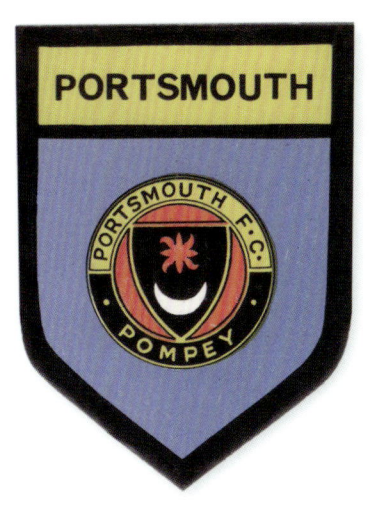

B.A.B. SOUVENIR CO. 1970.
Soccer Shields

Unknown number in series. Unnumbered. Pompey. (68 x 50mm), Portsmouth. (62 x 45mm).

B.A.B. SOUVENIR CO. 1971.
'Century' Series of Sticker Stamps

100 stamps. No. 6. Portsmouth. (24 x 30mm).

ESSO. 1972.
Esso Collection of Football Club Badges

76 badges. Unnumbered. Portsmouth. (32 x 30mm).

Given away with fuel purchases from Esso petrol stations. A gatefold folder was issued to house the collection.

WHITBREAD. 1970-79.
Whitbread Series

900+ matchbox labels. No. WW-413. Pompey. (54 x 35mm).

One of hundreds of matchbox labels, produced by Whitbread during the 1970s, documenting the firm's public houses. The sign which used to hang outside the Pompey pub on Frogmore Road displayed an image of Brian Lewis, a utility player who featured in almost every position during two spells with the club between 1963 and 1975.

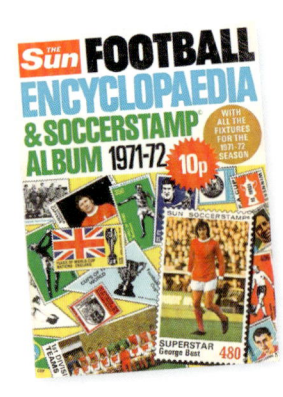

THE SUN. 1971/72.

Football Encyclopaedia & Soccerstamp Album 1971–72

500 stamps. No. 38. Club Crest. No. 48. Jimmy Dickinson. No. 98. FA Cup Winners 1939. No. 139. Team Group. No. 299. Jim Storrie. (Shown actual size).

Club captain Jim Storrie joined Pompey in December 1969, scoring 13 goals in 50 appearances before transferring to Aldershot.

THE CORNISH MATCH CO./ NSS NEWSAGENTS 1975.

Football Facts

50 matchbox labels. No. 15. Portsmouth. (35 x 50mm).

Pompey adopted a white shirt with two vertical blue stripes for three seasons between 1973 and 1976 following a fan competition to design a new kit.

THE SUN. 1978/79.

Soccercards

1,000 cards. No. 539. B. Wilson, No. 603. S. Foster, No. 779. S. Davey, No. 808. C. Garwood, No. 861. J. McIlwraith. (68 x 35mm).

A huge series of 1,000 *Soccercards* was released by The Sun during the 1978/79 season. Issued in packets of 50, these colourful hand-drawn portraits could be stuck into a variety of albums. The cards were divided into categories of International Stars, All Time Greats, Defenders, Midfielders and Strikers, plus Flags of Soccer Nations and Major Football Trophies. Jimmy Dickinson was included as an All Time Great. Billy Wilson, Steve Foster, Steve Davey, Colin Garwood and Jim McIlwraith were all part of the Fourth Division Pompey side which finished the 1978/79 season in seventh position.

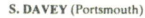

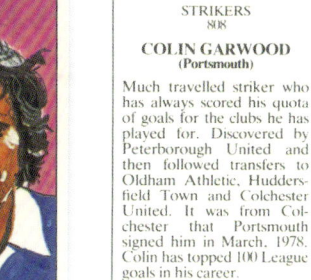

THE CLIMB BACK TO THE FIRST DIVISION

Frank Burrows' first season in charge brought immediate success with a fourth-place finish and promotion in 1979/80. Following almost two seasons back in the third tier, and with his team struggling in the lower reaches of the division, Burrows was replaced by Bobby Campbell who had represented Pompey both as a player and a coach during the 1960s. One of Campbell's first signings, Alan Biley, who had scored goals in the First Division for both Derby County and Everton, was an instant hit and his 23 league goals spearheaded Pompey's drive towards the 1982/83 Third Division title.

Chairman John Deacon funded the signing of England under-21 centre-forward Mark Hateley from Coventry City and he proved to be an ideal strike partner for Biley. They hit a combined total of 38 league goals in 1983/84 but a leaky defence left the side sitting in the bottom half of the table. Deacon, not for the first time, lost patience with his manager and Campbell was replaced by youth team coach Alan Ball in a caretaker capacity with one game remaining. Ball took full control for the 1984/85 season which started brightly but ultimately led to his side just missing out on a promotion place on goal difference to Manchester City.

The following season, despite looking like certainties for promotion throughout the campaign, Pompey fell short yet again, this time by three points. Deacon kept faith in his manager for the 1986/87 season and was repaid as Pompey's 28-year journey back to the First Division finally came to an end. A strong home record that included 17 wins, and a water-tight defence which leaked only 28 league goals, were key to their success. Mick Quinn finished the season as top scorer with 22 league goals.

Pompey's stay in the top-flight was to last just one season. Deacon's ambition to lead the club back to the top had been realised but, as his money ran out, the club's reins were handed to ex-QPR chairman Jim Gregory in June 1988.

1980-1989

PANINI. 1980/81.
Football 81

558 stickers. No. 449. Team. (49 x 65mm).

PANINI. 1981/82.
Football 82

516 stickers. No. 403. Team. (51 x 64mm).
401A. Badge. (51 x 32mm).

PANINI. 1983/84.
Football 84

526 stickers. No. 424. Team. (49 x 65mm).
423B. Badge. (47 x 32mm).

Panini was founded in 1961 by Italian brothers Benito and Giuseppe Panini who ran a newspaper distribution office. They began issuing football stickers and sold an astonishing 15 million packets during their first year.

When they entered the UK market in 1978, Panini's albums were an instant hit. By the mid-1980s, surveys suggested that over 90% of 9 to 11 year old boys were buying football stickers each year.

The albums featured double-page spreads of the top-flight teams that were made up of individual player portraits, team photos and foil club badges. Clubs in the lower divisions were usually limited to team photos and half-size foil club badges. The Football 83 album did not include clubs from the Third and Fourth divisions.

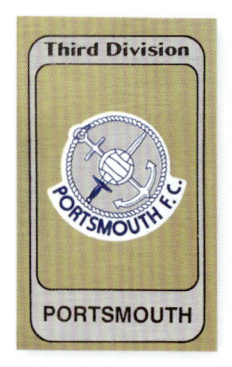

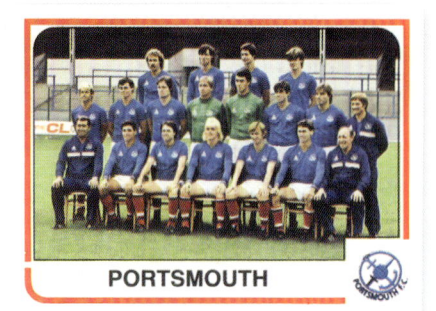

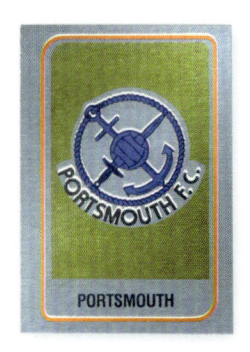

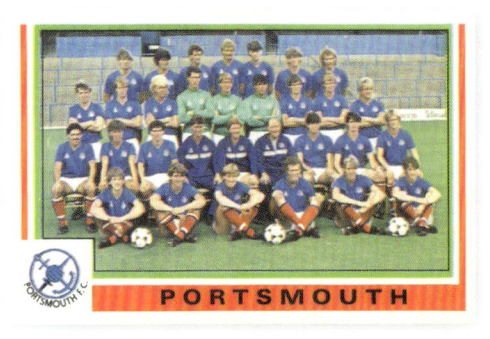

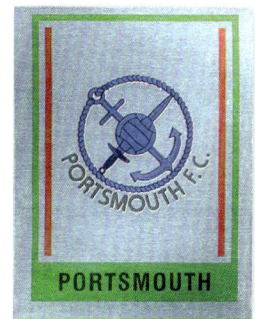

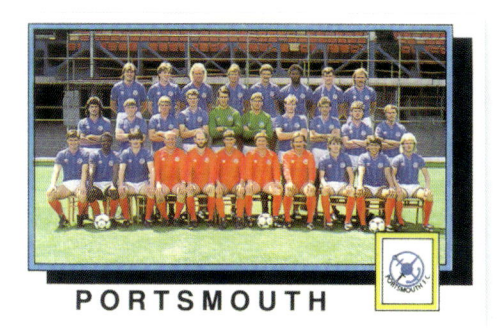

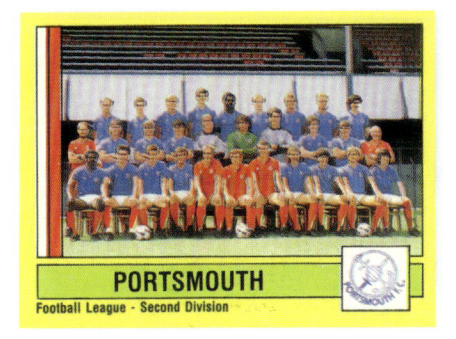

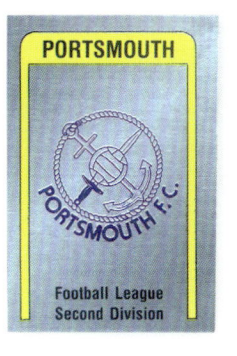

PANINI. 1984/85.

Football 85

535 stickers. No. 420. Team. (48 x 72mm). No. 419A. Badge. (48 x 36mm).

PANINI. 1985/86.

Football 86

574 stickers. No. 426. Team. (48 x 72mm). No. 427B. Badge. (48 x 36mm).

PANINI. 1986/87.

Football 87

576 stickers. No. 435. Team. (48 x 65mm). No. 436A. Badge. (48 x 32mm).

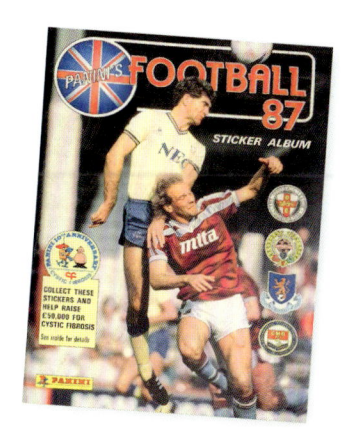

PANINI. 1983/84.

Football 84

526 stickers. No. 394. Alan Biley. (64 x 49mm).

Alan Biley featured in the Second Division All-Stars section of Panini's *Football 84* album. The popular striker scored 57 goals in 119 league and cup appearances, with two of his most memorable goals coming during a top-of-the-table clash with Oxford United at Fratton Park on December 22nd 1984. A supporter dressed as Santa had run onto the pitch during the second half. With Pompey trailing 1-0, in the time added on for the hold up in play, Biley managed to score two headed goals to seal a dramatic win.

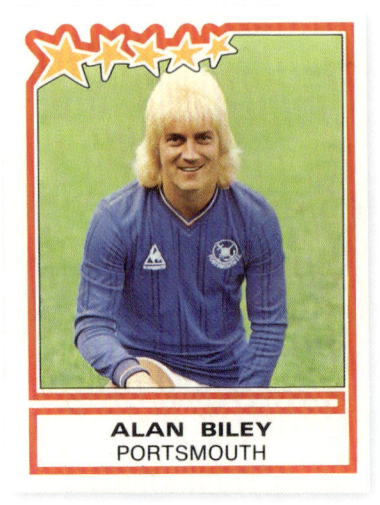

MATCH. 1984.

Goals and Goalscorers

70 cards. No. 10. Alan Biley. (98 x 74mm).

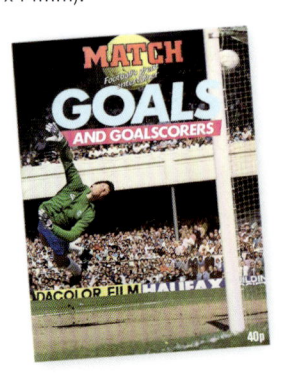

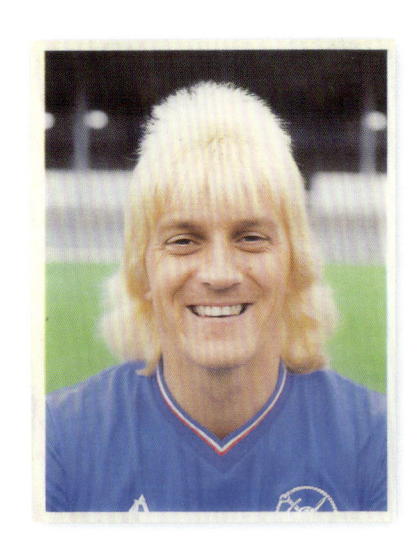

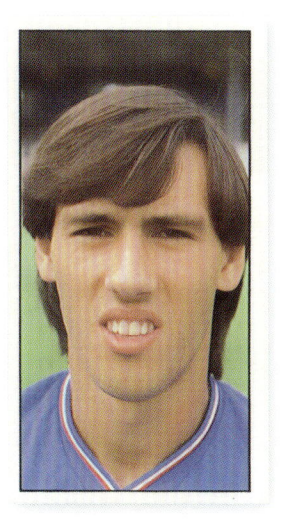

GEO. BASSETT & CO. (BARRATT DIVISION). 1984/85.
Football

50 cards. No. 3. Mark Hateley. (65 x 34mm).

A record £190,000 signing from Coventry City at the start of the 1983/84 season, Mark Hateley scored 25 goals in 44 appearances, including two hat-tricks, and was named Pompey's Player of the Year. His goalscoring form was noted at international level when he became the first Portsmouth player since Jimmy Dickinson to represent England with an appearance as a substitute versus the USSR. A goal against Brazil at the Maracana during England's summer tour of South America alerted several top clubs and he eventually moved to AC Milan for a record fee of £1 million.

GEO. BASSETT & CO. 1986/87.
Football

48 cards. No. 44. Nicky Morgan. (65 x 34mm).

Nicky Morgan joined Pompey from West Ham United in 1983 towards the end of the Third Division championship-winning campaign. He gained the tag 'Super Sub' after scoring seven goals in nine games, including three from the bench. Morgan moved to Stoke City during the 1986/87 season having made 107 league and cup appearances, scoring 34 goals.

UPEC MATCHES. 1981.
Football League Club Series

92 matchbox labels. No. 63. Portsmouth. (49 x 33mm).

SWIZZELS-MATLOW. 1986/87.
Soccer Shields

68 stickers. No. 38. Portsmouth. (45 x 32mm).

Confectionery firm Swizzels-Matlow issued a collection of *Soccer Shields* inside packets of Refreshers sweets throughout the 1986/87 season.

GEO. BASSETT & CO. 1987/88.
Football

48 cards. No. 29. Portsmouth FC. (34 x 65mm).

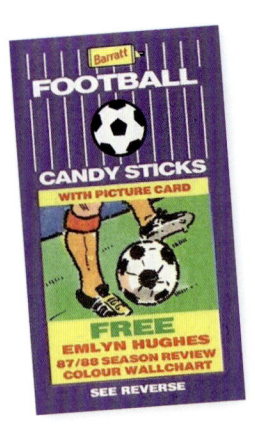

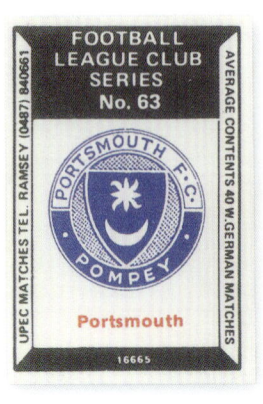

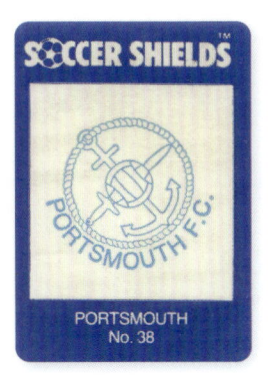

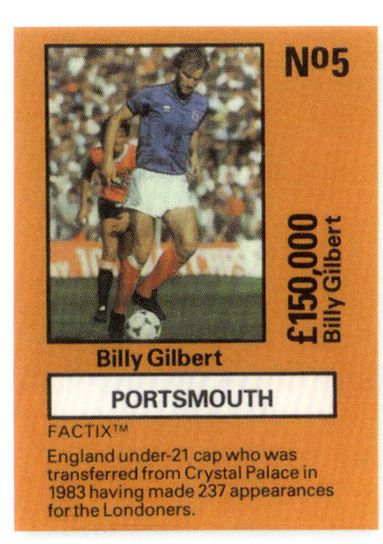

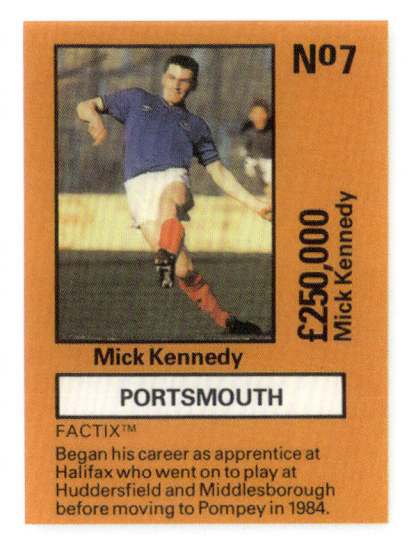

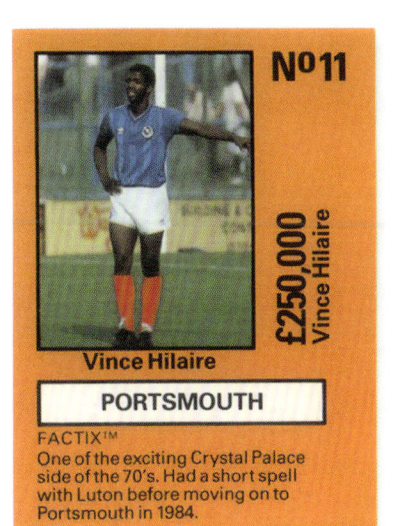

BOSS LEISURE. 1987.

Emlyn Hughes' Team Tactix

275 cards. No. 1. Alan Knight, No. 2. Kenny Swain, No. 3. Paul Hardyman, No. 4. Noel Blake, No. 5. Billy Gilbert, No. 6. Mick Tait, No. 7. Mick Kennedy, No. 8. Kevin Dillon, No. 9. Paul Mariner, No. 10. Mick Quinn, No. 11. Vince Hilaire. (69 x 49mm).

Emlyn Hughes' Team Tactix included 275 cards, featuring 11 players from each of the top clubs in the English and Scottish leagues.

Centre-back Billy Gilbert, midfielder Mick Kennedy and winger Vince Hilaire were all members of the sides that narrowly missed out on promotion to the First Division in 1985 and 1986, before eventually succeeding in 1987, the year this board game was released.

Billy Gilbert, a £100,000 signing from Crystal Palace in 1984, made 159 appearances before joining Colchester United in October 1989.

Mick Kennedy was a key member of Pompey's First Division side when he was sold for £250,000 to Second Division Bradford City in January 1988 against the wishes of manager Alan Ball.

Vince Hilaire made 44 appearances in 1987/88 ahead of a £190,000 transfer to Leeds United. Spells with Stoke City and Exeter City followed before he joined Southern League side Waterlooville in the summer of 1992 as joint player-manager along with ex-teammate Gilbert.

PANINI. 1987/88.
Football 88

574 stickers. No. 213. Badge, No. 214. Noel Blake, No. 220. Alan Ball. (65 x 53mm). *Complete list can be found on page 196.*

A place in the First Division saw Pompey featured on a double-page spread in a Panini sticker album for the first time in *Football 88*.

Centre-back Noel Blake signed from Birmingham City in the summer of 1984 and quickly became a fans' favourite, winning two consecutive Player of the Season awards in 1985/86 and 1986/87. He joined Leeds United in 1988 having made 168 league and cup appearances, scoring 13 goals.

World Cup winner Alan Ball had two spells as manager at Fratton Park. First appointed in 1984, he guided the club to promotion to the top-flight in 1987. Following a single season in the First Division Pompey were relegated and Ball was sacked in January 1989 as his side struggled to mount a challenge for promotion. He returned in February 1998 with Pompey several points adrift at the foot of the Nationwide First Division but successfully steered the side to safety following a 3-1 victory at Bradford City on the final day of the season.

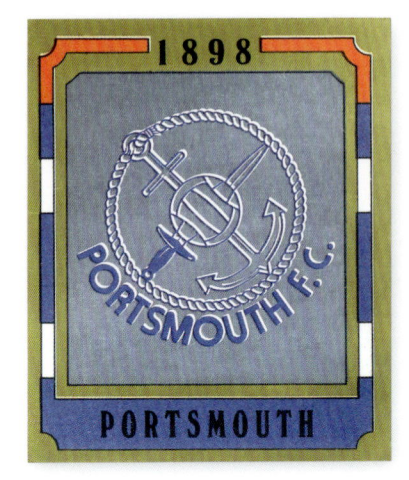

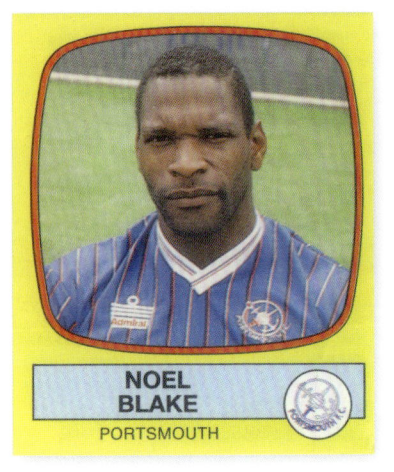

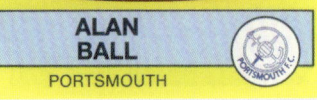

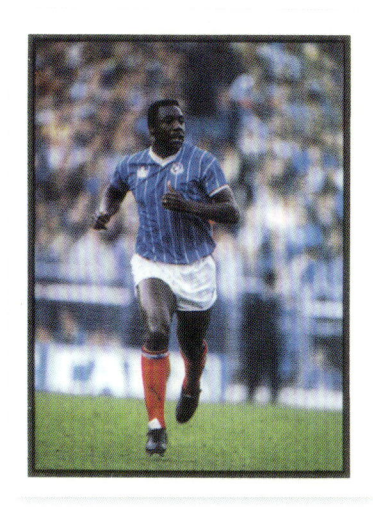

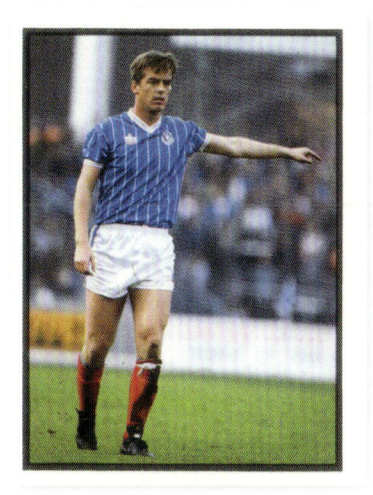

DAILY MIRROR. 1987/88.
Soccer 88

360 stickers. No. 190. Paul Mariner, No. 191. Terry Connor, No. 194. Kevin Dillon. (65 x 48mm). *Complete list can be found on page 196.*

The Daily Mirror issued their second and final sticker album for the 1987/88 season. *Soccer 88*'s format loosely followed Panini's tried and tested formula, with each club allocated a spread. The player images were a combination of portrait and action shots, and the manager and club captain featured on foil stickers.

Centre-forward Paul Mariner signed from Arsenal on a free transfer in 1986, partnering Mick Quinn during the 1986/87 promotion campaign, and scored Pompey's first top-flight goal since 1959 during the 4-2 defeat away to Oxford United in August 1987.

Terry Connor spent four seasons at Brighton & Hove Albion before joining Pompey in 1987. The centre-forward scored 16 goals in 56 appearances then signed for Swansea City in 1990.

Kevin Dillon's six-year spell at Pompey saw the club rise from the Third to the First Division, and drop back down to the Second. The team's regular penalty-taker, he once scored a hat-trick from the spot during a 3-2 Full Members Cup win against Millwall at Fratton Park.

MATCH. 1987/88.
The FA Cup Sticker Album 1988

64 stickers. No. 19. Ian Baird. (74 x 50mm).

One of several sticker collections given away with Match magazine during this period, sheets of stickers were issued weekly to complete the album.

A record £285,000 summer signing from Leeds United, Ian Baird's short stay with Pompey brought a return of just one goal in 22 appearances.

MATCH. 1987/88.
Match Fact Football Yearbook 1987/88

24 cut-out stickers. Unnumbered. Mick Quinn. (94 x 72mm).

MATCH. 1987/88.
The Match Winners Series

30 cards. No. 13. Portsmouth. (53 x 82mm).

Issued as perforated sheets of 10 cards.

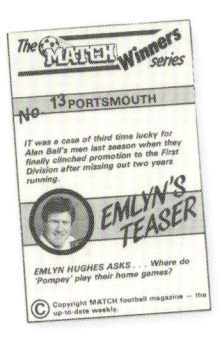

LEAF. 1987/88.
100 Years of Soccer Stars

100 stickers. No. 32. Mike Channon. (98 x 74mm).

Issued by Leaf during the 1987/88 season to commemorate the centenary of the Football League. Former England striker Mick Channon spent the majority of his career at Southampton before he joined Pompey in 1985.

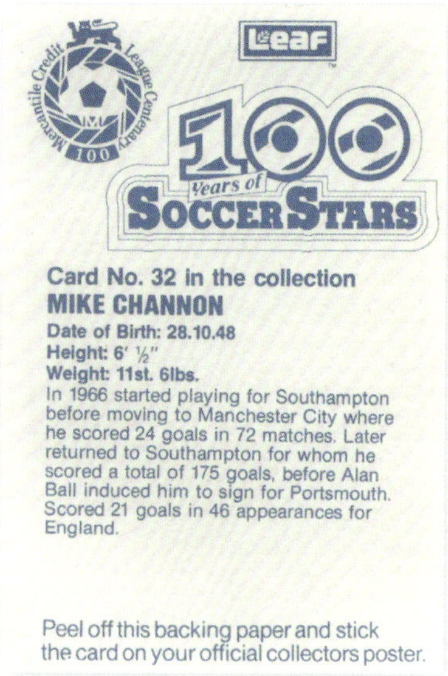

MATCH. 1988.
Match Fact Football Yearbook Sticker Stars 1988/89

48 stickers. Unnumbered. Mick Quinn. (54 x 46mm).

Striker Mick Quinn joined Pompey from Oldham Athletic for £150,000 in March 1986 and his 22 league goals the following season helped fire Pompey to promotion. He scored 64 goals in 135 league and cup appearances before moving to Newcastle United for £650,000 in 1989.

TOPPS. 1989.
The Saint 'n' Greavsie All Star Football Collection

207 stickers. No. 49. Kenny Swain. (54 x 38mm).

Signed from Nottingham Forest on a free transfer in 1985, full-back Kenny Swain captained Pompey to promotion in 1986/87. Originally issued as a pair with Wales international Kevin Ratcliffe.

FA CUP AND PROMOTION HEARTBREAK

During the early 1990s, under the guidance of manager Jim Smith, Pompey narrowly missed out on both a place in the FA Cup Final and promotion to the newly-formed Premier League. Two epic FA Cup semi-final contests with Liverpool in April 1992 had failed to separate the sides after extra-time. In the first game at Highbury, Ronnie Whelan broke Pompey hearts with a late equaliser after Darren Anderton had put his side 1-0 up with just six minutes remaining. The replay at Villa Park finished 0-0 and in losing the resulting penalty shoot-out, Pompey were desperately unlucky not to progress to the final.

A tremendous run of form towards the end of the 1992/93 season, aided by the record-breaking goalscoring exploits of striker Guy Whittingham, left Pompey needing four points from their remaining two fixtures to secure promotion. A dreadful performance versus Sunderland at Roker Park saw Pompey lose 4-1 and finish the game with nine men as Guy Butters and Paul Walsh were both sent off. The final match against Grimsby Town brought a 2-1 win but West Ham's 2-0 victory over Cambridge United saw the east Londoners promoted in second-place on goals scored. Pompey lost the resulting play-off semi-final to Leicester City over two legs and were left facing another season in the second tier, the newly-formed Football League Division One.

The sale of Whittingham to Aston Villa the following summer, and Walsh to Manchester City in March 1994, inevitably diminished Pompey's goalscoring threat and the team finished the 1993/94 season a disappointing 17th. Two more seasons of struggle culminated in a relegation battle in 1995/96 when a 1-0 final-day victory at Huddersfield Town kept Pompey up. Two years later Alan Ball, who had returned as manager in January 1998, steered his side to yet another last-gasp escape from the drop with a 3-1 win at Bradford City's Valley Parade.

1990–1999

VICTORY BLEND. 1990.

Jolly Jack's Mixture – 1940s

20 cards. No. 1. Jimmy Aslett, No. 2. Len Phillips, No. 3. Ike Clarke, No. 4. Reg Flewin, No. 5. Fred 'Flash' Evans, No. 6. Bill Hindmarsh, No. 7. Gordon Neave, No. 8. Ernie Butler, No. 9. Jasper Yeuell, No. 10. Duggie Reid, No. 11. Phil Rookes, No. 12. Jack Froggatt, No. 13. Bill Butler, No. 14. Peter Harris, No. 15. Jim Scoular, No. 16. Jim Dickinson, No. 17. Jack Emery, No. 18. Lindy Delapenha, No. 19. Ron Humpston, No. 20. Bert Barlow. (62 x 42mm).

A retrospective series produced in 1990 featuring players who had represented Pompey during the 1940s. Victory Blend collections were sometimes issued as framed sets.

Lloyd Lindberg 'Lindy' Delapenha was recommended to Pompey while serving in the Army and the Kingston-born forward was the first Jamaican to play professional football in England. His debut came in a 1-1 draw versus Blackpool at Fratton Park in November 1948 and he made a further eight league and cup appearances throughout the championship seasons before a move to Middlesbrough in April 1950. It was during his eight-year stay at Ayresome Park that he made his name, scoring 93 goals in 270 appearances. After retiring from the game, Delapenha became Director of Sport for the Jamaican Broadcasting Corporation.

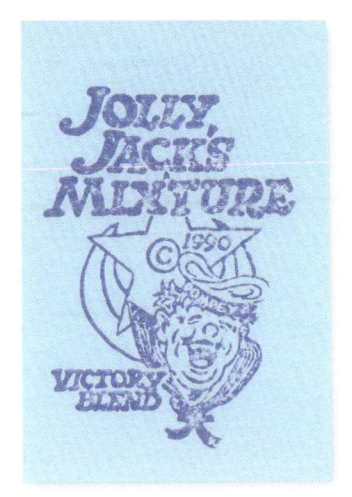

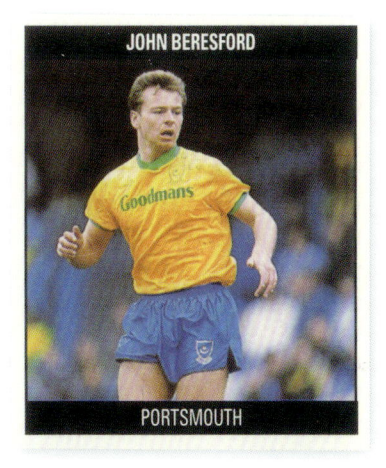

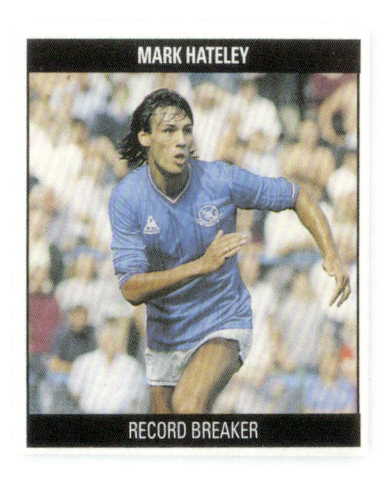

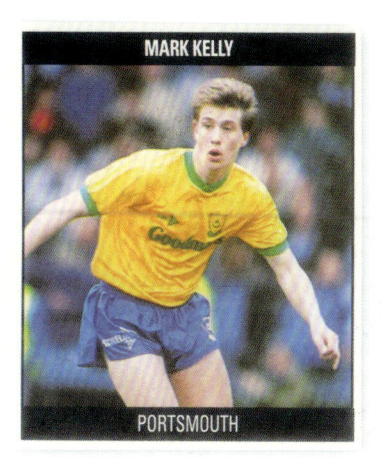

ORBIS. 1990/91.

The Orbis Football Sticker Album

630 stickers. No. G26. Alan Knight, No. F13. John Beresford, No. F68. Warren Neill, No. W9. Mark Chamberlain, No. D90. Gary Stevens, No. D35. Graeme Hogg, No. W24. Mark Kelly, No. S20. Terry Connor, No. S16. Colin Clarke, No. RB33. Mark Hateley. (65 x 54mm).

The Orbis Football Sticker Album covered the top three divisions of both the English and Scottish leagues. The collection was divided into sections of Managers, Strikers, Midfielders, Wingers, Defenders, Full Backs and Goalkeepers and Record Breakers. Nine members of Pompey's 1990/91 squad featured, including left-back John Beresford a £300,000 signing from Barnsley in 1989, and Mark Kelly, an Irish winger who was described by manager Alan Ball as "the next George Best". Kelly made 55 appearances before a serious knee injury forced him to retire in 1992. He later returned to Fratton Park as Pompey's Under-18s manager.

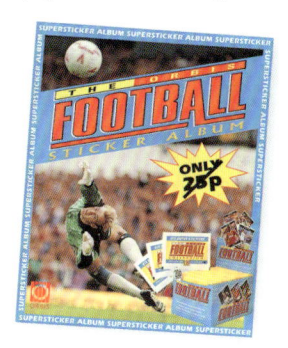

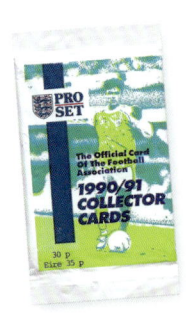

PRO SET. 1990/91.

Footballers

328 cards. No. 287. Alan Knight, No. 288. Gary Stevens, No. 289. Mark Chamberlain. (88 x 64mm).

American firm Pro Set was successful in the NFL Football and NHL Hockey trading card market in the late 1980s and early 90s. Their first UK football cards series was released during the 1990/91 season and featured both First and Second Division clubs.

Gary Stevens signed from Tottenham Hotspur, initially on loan, in 1990 and went on to make 58 league and cup appearances in both midfield and central defence. A knee injury sustained at Plymouth Argyle's Home Park the following year ended his playing career.

Mark Chamberlain, a £200,000 buy from Sheffield Wednesday, spent six seasons at Pompey between 1988 and 1994. A skilful winger, he scored a number of memorable goals during his 189 appearances before moving to Brighton & Hove Albion on a free transfer.

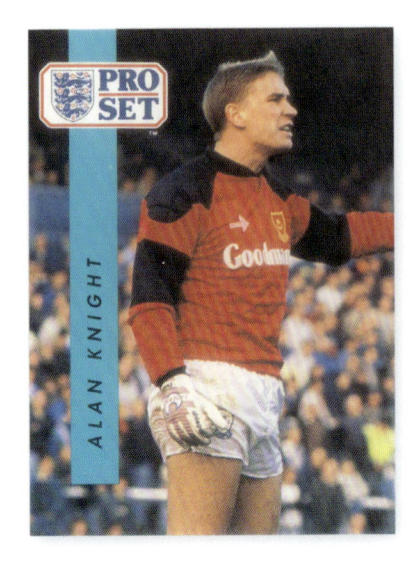

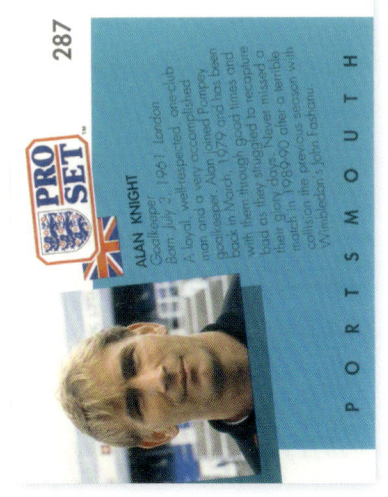

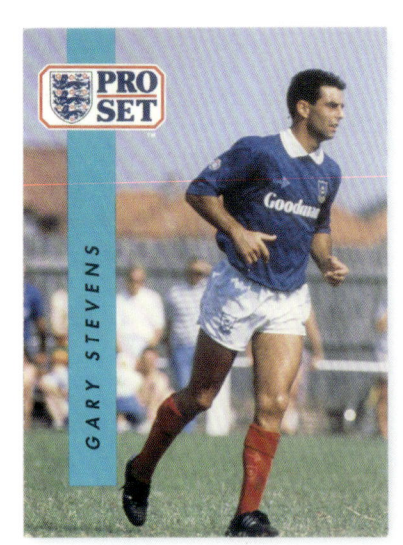

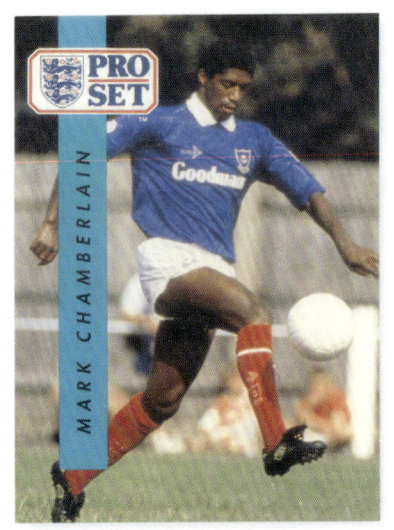

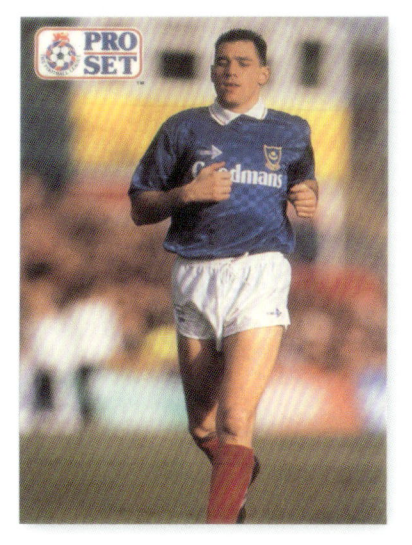

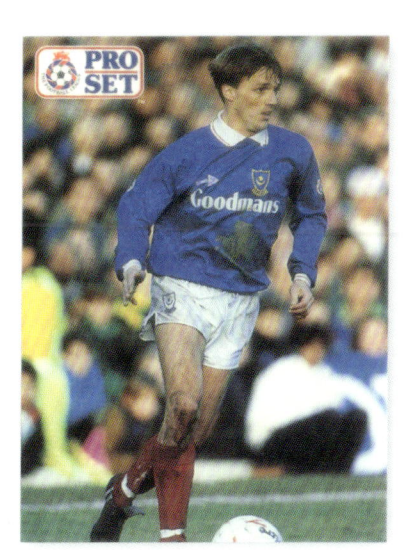

PRO SET. 1991/92.

Footballers (Division 2, Part 1)

230 cards. No. 191. Guy Whittingham, No. 192. Colin Clarke, No. 193. Warren Aspinall, No. 194. Steve Wigley. (88 x 64mm).

Pro Set's second series was issued in two parts for the 1991/92 season and included six Portsmouth players.

Winger Steve Wigley was signed from non-league Curzon Ashton by Brian Clough for Nottingham Forest as a 21-year-old. He moved to Sheffield United, then Birmingham City, before John Gregory brought him to Fratton Park in 1989 for £300,000. Wigley was released at the end of the 1991/92 season having made 137 appearances.

The Darren Anderton card in Part 2 of the series incorrectly features images of defender Kit Symons. Southampton-born Anderton began his career as an apprentice at Fratton Park, making his senior debut versus Wolverhampton Wanderers in November 1990. He made his name during the 1992 FA Cup Fourth Round tie against Leyton Orient, hitting two spectacular goals in a 2-0 win and scored his most memorable Pompey goal in the semi-final versus Liverpool at Highbury. He was sold to Tottenham Hotspur the following summer for £1.7m having scored 13 goals in 74 appearances.

1990–1999 | 153

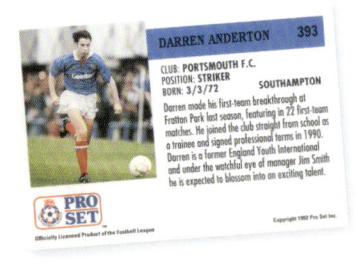

PRO SET. 1991/92.

Footballers (Division 2, Part 2)

294 cards. No. 392. Mark Chamberlain, No. 393. Darren Anderton (error card, Kit Symons pictured). (88 x 64mm).

PRO SET. 1991/92.

Fixtures Cards

100 cards. No. 39. Guy Whittingham/ Portsmouth's Fixture List. (88 x 64mm).

Ex-Corporal Guy Whittingham bought himself out of the Army for £450 before arriving at Fratton Park in the summer of 1989. He scored 42 league goals during the 1992/93 season to surpass Billy Haines' long-standing club record, as Pompey were narrowly beaten to promotion by West Ham United. He moved to Aston Villa following 101 goals in 179 games.

Whittingham returned for a second spell, initially on loan, from Sheffield Wednesday in January 1999, scoring 11 goals in 37 appearances. He played his final match for Pompey on Boxing Day 2000 and later managed the club between November 2012 and November 2013.

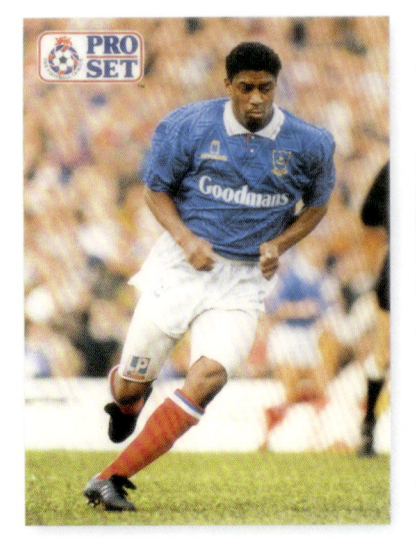

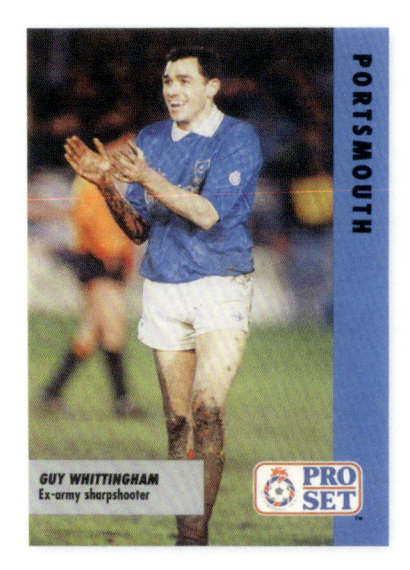

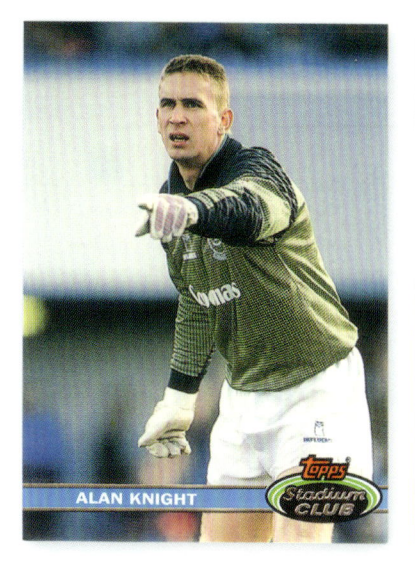

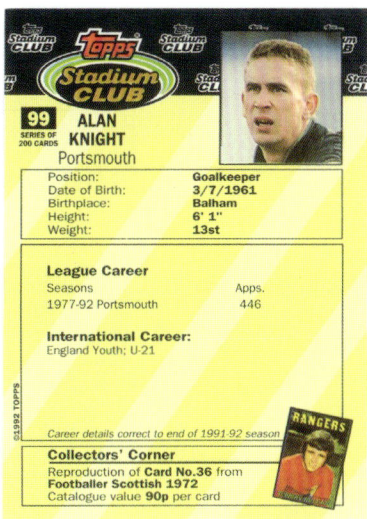

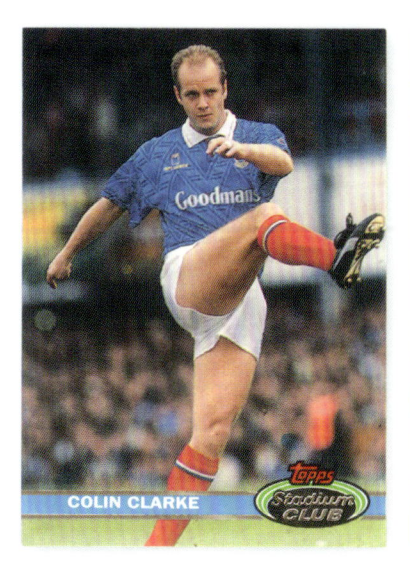

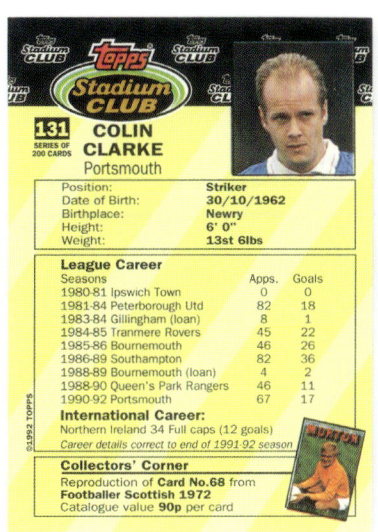

TOPPS. 1992/93.
Stadium Club

200 cards. No. 99. Alan Knight, No. 131. Colin Clarke. (90 x 65mm).

American firm Topps had produced baseball, basketball, ice-hockey and American football gum cards since the 1950s and entered the UK market in 1975 following a takeover of A&BC.

Known simply as 'Legend' at Fratton Park, Alan Knight holds the goalkeeping record for league appearances with one club, and is second only to Jimmy Dickinson in total number of appearances for Pompey. It was Dickinson who gave Knight his debut at the age of 16, on the final day of the 1977/78 season at Rotherham United, in a side already relegated to the Fourth Division. He served Pompey through four decades, and all four divisions, during his 23 seasons with the club. His 801st and last appearance came against Norwich City at Carrow Road on 3rd January 2000. He represented England under-21s on two occasions and was awarded the MBE in the 2001 New Year Honours list.

Colin Clarke became Pompey's record signing when he joined from Queens Park Rangers for £400,000 in May 1990. The Northern Ireland striker, who made 38 appearances for his country, scored 26 goals in 102 appearances before an injury sustained in the early part of the 1992/93 season ended his career.

PANINI. 1994/95.

Football League 95

600 stickers. No. 184. Team, No. 185. Alan Knight, No. 186. Andy Awford, No. 187. Jon Gittens, No. 188. Warren Neill, No. 189. Robbie Pethick, No. 190. Kits from the past, No. 191. Mark Stimson, No. 192. Kit Symons, No. 193. Badge, No. 194. Alan McLoughlin, No. 195. Gerry Creaney, No. 196. Paul Hall, No. 197. Darryl Powell, No. 198. Predrag Radosavljevic. (69 x 54mm).

Having lost the rights to English football's top division to Merlin Publishing with the inception of the Premier League in 1992, the *Football League 95* album saw Panini's attention turn to the Football League.

Darryl Powell began his career as a trainee at Fratton Park, making his debut in February 1989. He moved to Derby County in 1995 for £750,000, and represented Jamaica at the 1998 World Cup in France alongside Pompey's Paul Hall and Fitzroy Simpson.

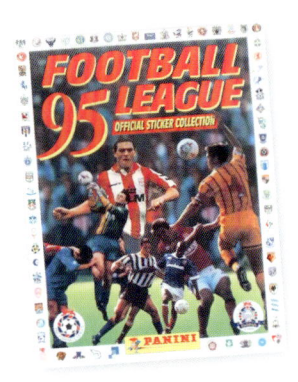

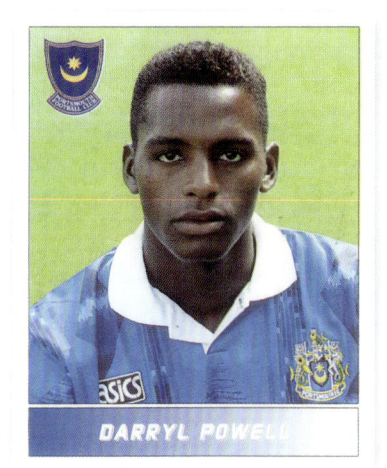

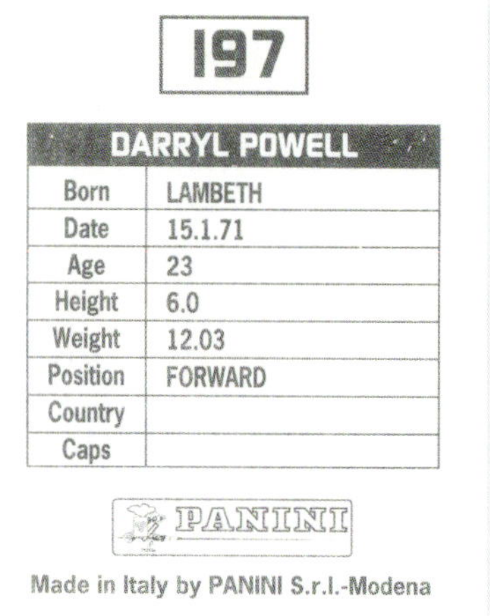

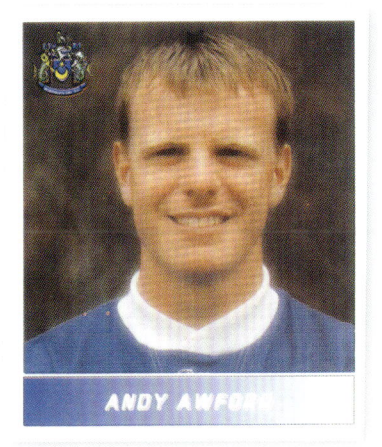

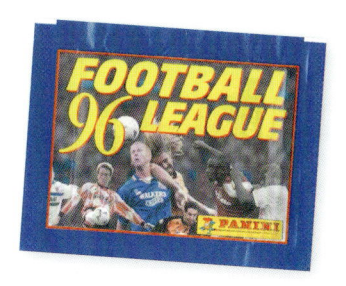

PANINI. 1995/96.
Football League 96

468 stickers. No. 197. Team, No. 198. Alan Knight, No. 199. Andy Awford, No. 200. Guy Butters, No. 201. Lee Russell, No. 202. Mark Stimson, No. 203. Jimmy Carter, No. 204. Badge, No. 205. Alan McLoughlin, No. 206. Robbie Pethick, No. 207. John Durnin, No. 208. Paul Hall, No. 209. Jason Rees, No. 210. Paul Walsh. (65 x 54mm).

At 16 years of age, centre-back Andy Awford became the youngest player to appear for Pompey in a league match, away to Crystal Palace in 1989. He formed a solid central-defensive partnership with Kit Symons that conceded just nine league goals at home during the 1992/93 season.

He suffered a broken leg in September 1994 but recovered to make a total of 361 appearance before retiring in 2000 aged 28. Awford later served the club as chief scout, reserve team manager, caretaker manager and finally, between May 2014 and April 2015, first team manager.

VICTORY BLEND. 1995.

Pompey's Pride

11 cards. No. 1. Jasper Yeuell, No. 2. Ernie Butler, No. 3. Harry Ferrier, No. 4. Jim Scoular, No. 5. Reg Flewin, No. 6. Jimmy Dickinson, No. 7. Peter Harris, No. 8. Duggie Reid, No. 9. Ike Clarke, No. 10. Len Phillips, No. 11. Jack Froggatt. (64 x 37mm).

Another retrospective series by Victory Blend, this time celebrating the 1948/49 championship-winning side.

Jasper Yeuell was discovered by chief scout Bob Jackson playing in the Army and made his debut at home to Arsenal on Boxing Day 1946. He made a total of 36 league and cup appearances, 16 of which came during the championship seasons, before transferring to Barnsley in 1952. Yeuell played 19 matches for the Yorkshire club before he was forced to retire through injury at the age of 27.

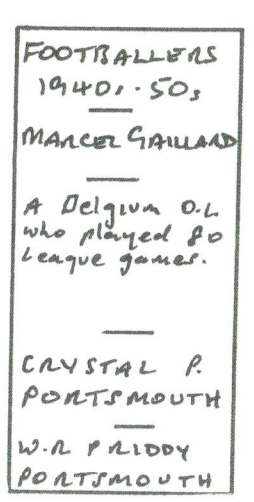

W.R. PRIDDY. 1996.

Footballers 1940s–50s

1,100 cards. Nos. 1–1000 Footballers, Nos. 1001–1088 International Squads, Nos. 1089–1099 Great Britain, No. 1100 Unknown. No. 322. Marcel Gaillard, No. 1030. Derek Dougan, No. 1092. Jimmy Dickinson. (74 x 40mm). *Complete list can be found on page 196.*

A series of 1,100 hand-drawn cards featuring footballers of the 1940s and 1950s, issued by Bill Priddy in 1996. Eighty-one of the cards feature players who represented Pompey during their career.

Belgian outside-left Marcel Gaillard joined Pompey from Crystal Palace in 1951, taking over the number 11 shirt from Jack Froggatt who switched to centre-half. He made 64 appearances, scoring 13 goals, before joining Southern League club Weymouth in 1951.

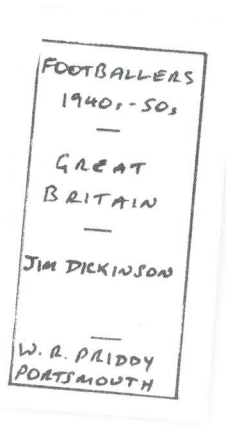

PANINI. 1996/97.

1st Division 1997

384 stickers. No. 245. Badge, No. 246. Alan Knight, No. 247. Andy Awford, No. 248. Guy Butters, No. 249. Lee Russell, No. 250. Andy Thomson, No. 251. Rory Allen, No. 252. Jimmy Carter, No. 253. Alan McLoughlin, No. 254. Robbie Pethick, No. 255. Fitzroy Simpson, No. 256. John Durnin, No. 257. Paul Hall, No. 258. Jason Rees. (76 x 54mm).

Former Liverpool apprentice John Durnin signed from Oxford United for £200,000. Known for his tireless work rate, he made 198 league and cup appearances for Pompey as both a striker and midfielder between 1993 and 2000, scoring 33 goals.

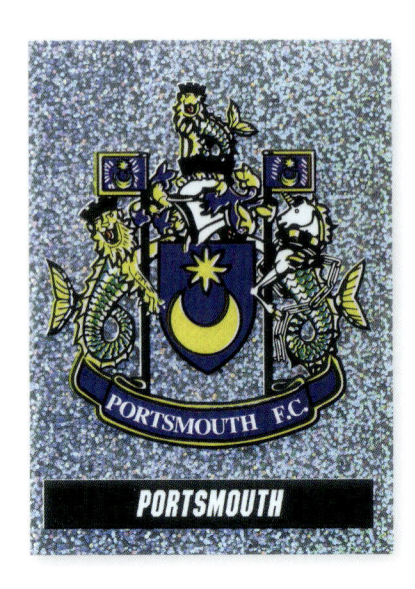

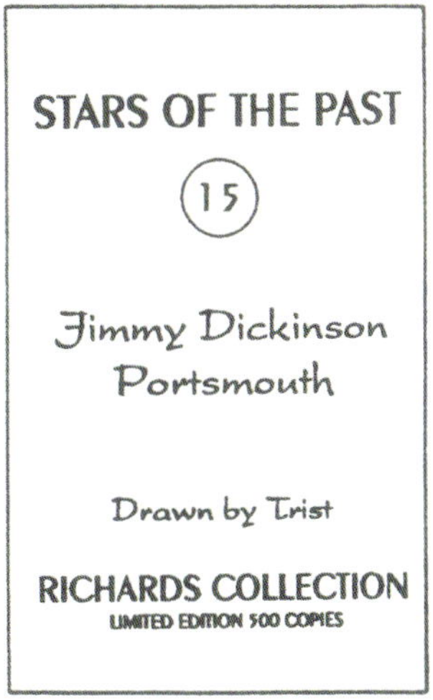

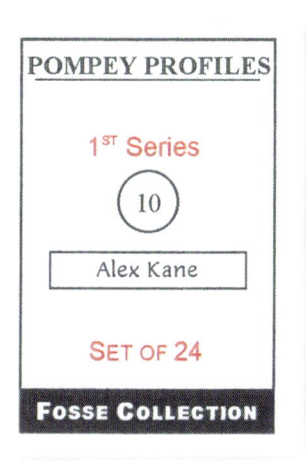

Several Richards Collection and Fosse Collection series were issued during the 1990s. The caricatures featured on these retrospective sets were drawn in a style which was popular among sports illustrators between the 1930s and 1950s.

RICHARDS COLLECTION. 1994.

Stars of the Past

21 cards. No. 15. Jimmy Dickinson, No. 21. Jimmy Scoular. (69 x 45mm).

FOSSE COLLECTION. 1998.

Pompey Profiles (1st Series)

24 cards. No. 1. Willie Beedie, No. 2. Bill Probert, No. 3. John Anderson, No. 4. Bill Bagley, No. 5. Harry Walker, No. 6. Bill Rochford, No. 7. Cliff Parker, No. 8. Fred Worrall, No. 9. Abe Smith, No. 10. Alex 'Sandy' Kane, No. 11. Willie 'Farmer' Haines, No. 12. Jimmy McAlinden, No. 13, Sep Rutherford, No. 14. Alec Mackie, No. 15. Freddie Cook, No. 16. Jock Gilfillan, No. 17. Guy Wharton, No. 18. Lew Morgan, No. 19. Arthur Groves, No. 20. Jack Weddle, No. 21. John McColgan, No. 22. James 'Smiler' Martin, No. 23. Harry Goodwin, No. 24. Dave Thackeray. (58 x 40mm).

Goalkeeper Alexander Kane signed from Heart of Midlothian in the summer of 1923 having spent the previous season on loan at Reading. He was ever-present as Pompey won the Third Division South championship in 1923/24.

THE PREMIER LEAGUE AND FA CUP GLORY

Pompey spent the first two seasons of the new century battling the drop. A 3-0 victory against Barnsley on the final day of the 2000/01 season saw Huddersfield Town relegated at Pompey's expense. Chairman Milan Mandaric, who had taken control at Pompey in May 1999, brought Yugoslavia and Croatia international Robert Prosinecki to Fratton Park ahead of the 2001/02 season and his creativity, combined with the goals of Peter Crouch, saved Pompey from relegation a second time. Mandaric installed director of football Harry Redknapp as manager in March 2002 and the following season he led Pompey to the First Division title.

Having finished in 13th and 16th place during their first two seasons in the Premier League, Pompey narrowly avoided relegation in 2005/06. Eight points adrift of safety at the end of February, Pompey embarked on a run of six wins and two draws from the final nine games including a 2-1 victory at Wigan Athletic which ensured safety with a game to spare. At the end of the season Alexandre Gaydamak, who had purchased a 50% stake in the club in January 2006, became the sole owner, and soon embarked on a spending spree which initially brought success, but that ultimately risked the future of the club.

The high-calibre squad assembled by Redknapp achieved an 8th place finish in 2007/08, the highest league position since 1955, and FA Cup glory for the second time with a 1-0 win versus Cardiff City. The run to the final included a stunning 1-0 defeat of Premier League champions Manchester United at Old Trafford. Kanu's solitary goals secured both the semi-final and final victories at Wembley. The FA Cup triumph brought with it qualification to the UEFA Cup and, as Pompey played out a 2-2 draw with Italian giants AC Milan at Fratton Park, the club appeared to be on an upward trajectory.

By the summer of 2009, however, Pompey were in a perilous financial position. Gaydamak sold the club to Emirati businessman Sulaiman Al-Fahim who became the first in a succession of owners who failed to turn Pompey's finances around.

2000–2010

MERLIN. 2003/04.

F.A. Premier League 2003/2004 Season Pocket Collection

162 stickers. No. 132. Hayden Foxe, No. 133. Arjan De Zeeuw, No. 134. Matthew Taylor, No. 135. Nigel Quashie, No. 138. Svetoslav Todorov. (59 x 25mm and 42 x 30mm). *Complete list can be found on page 196.*

Merlin Publishing Ltd. was founded in 1989 and quickly became a major player in the European collectible stickers and cards market. In 1995 the firm was acquired by Topps, who continued to use the Merlin brand name.

Australia international centre-back Hayden Foxe joined Pompey from West Ham United in May 2002. He featured regularly in the side promoted to the Premier League in 2003, and during the first few months of the 2003/04 campaign, before a fractured foot ruled him out at Christmas. Foxe struggled to overcome the injury and was eventually released by manager Alain Perrin in June 2005.

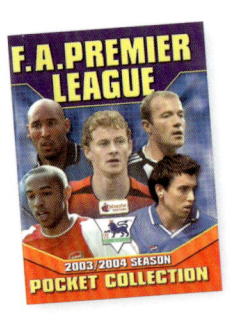

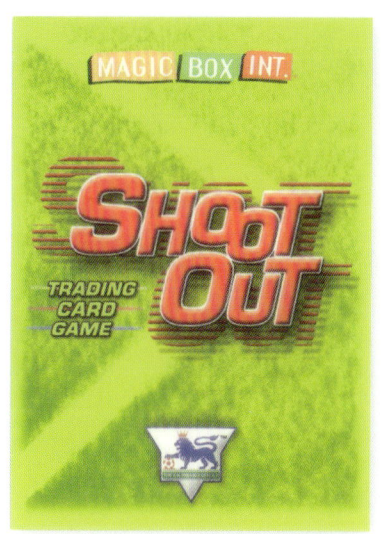

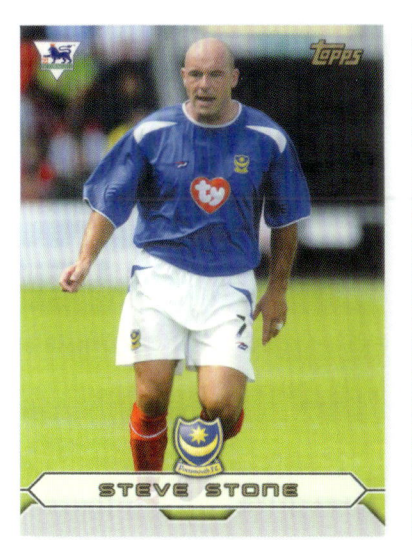

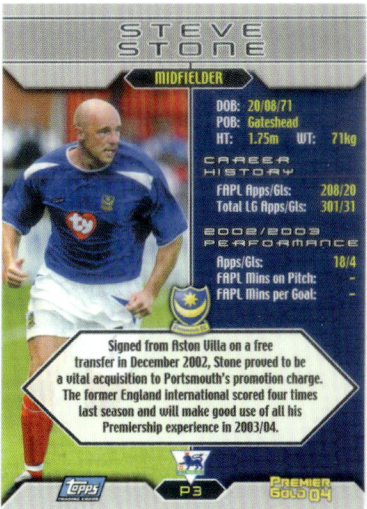

MAGIC BOX INTERNATIONAL. 2003/04.

Shoot Out Trading Card Game 2003–2004

360 cards. Unnumbered. Boris Zivkovic. (87 x 61mm). *Complete list can be found on page 196.*

Magic Box International produced *Shoot Out Trading Card Game* cards across four seasons between 2003 and 2007.

Boris Zivkovic, a 2002 Champions League finalist, brought a wealth of European experience to Pompey when he signed from Bayer Leverkusen in the summer of 2003. A falling-out with manager Harry Redknapp the following December, however, meant the Croatia international's stay at Fratton Park was short-lived and he was released having made just 20 appearances.

TOPPS. 2003/04.

Premier Gold 2004

225 cards. No. P3. Steve Stone. (89 x 64mm). *Complete list can be found on page 196.*

Initially signed on loan from Aston Villa, England international Steve Stone's vast experience benefitted Pompey for three seasons between 2002 and 2005. He was a key member of the side which won promotion to the Premier League and helped the team narrowly avoid relegation in 2005. Stone was released at the end of the 2004/05 season, joining Leeds United.

MERLIN. 2003/04.

Merlin's F.A. Premier League 04 Official Sticker Collection – Autograph Edition

578 stickers. No. 471. Shaka Hislop. (68 x 54mm). *Complete list can be found on page 196.*

Shaka Hislop arrived at Fratton Park from West Ham United in 2002. He was ever-present during the First Division title-winning campaign of 2002/2003 and made a total of 100 league and cup appearances before re-joining The Hammers in January 2005. Hislop's 26 international appearances for Trinidad and Tobago included their first-ever World Cup Finals match in 2006.

GRAMAL. 2004.

Zvezde Evropskog Fudbala 2004

216 stickers. No. 106. Boris Zivkovic, No. 142. Svetoslav Todorov, No. 157. Alexei Smertin. (67 x 48mm).

Issued in Serbia ahead of the Euro 2004 tournament, Gramal's *Zvezde Evropskog Fudbala 2004* album featured a selection of top European football stars.

Signed on loan from Chelsea during the 2003/04 season, Alexei Smertin made 33 league and cup appearances for Pompey. Following some impressive performances, the skilful midfielder returned to his parent club where he collected a Premier League winners' medal in 2005.

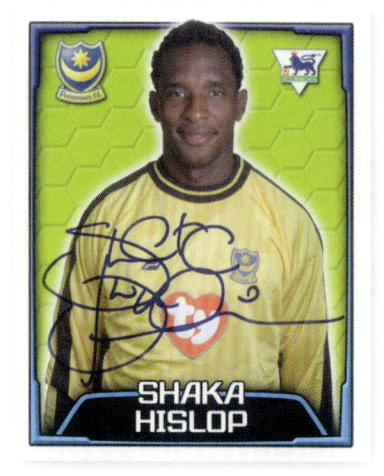

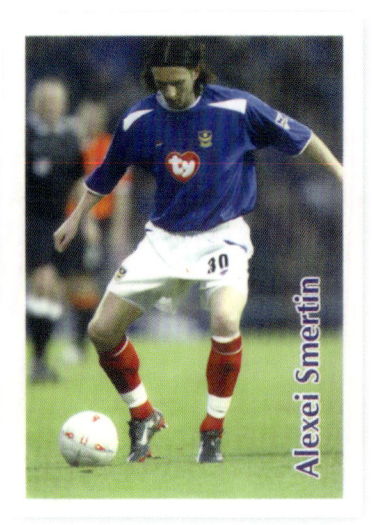

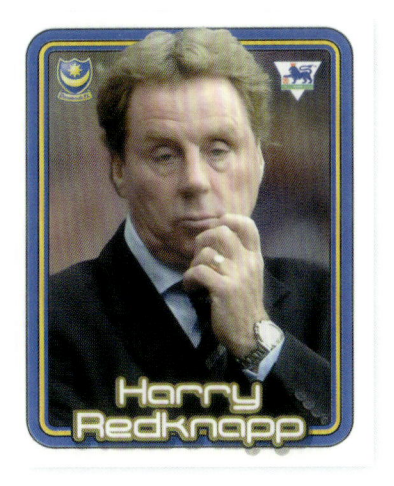

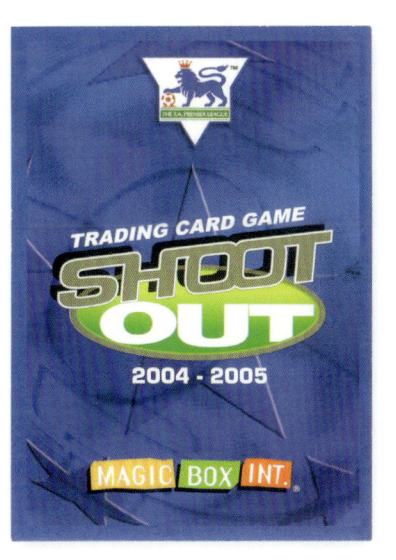

MERLIN. 2004/05.

Merlin's F.A. Premier League 05 Official Sticker Collection

574 stickers. No. 487. Harry Redknapp. (68 x 54mm). *Complete list can be found on page 197.*

During two spells in charge at Fratton Park, manager Harry Redknapp oversaw promotion to the Premier League in 2003, the 2008 FA Cup triumph and the club's highest league finish since the 1950s. His resignation and subsequent move to Southampton in 2004 made him unpopular with large sections of Pompey's supporters, but he was reappointed in December 2005. Redknapp resigned for a second time in October 2008 before taking over at Tottenham Hotspur.

MAGIC BOX INTERNATIONAL. 2004/05.

Shoot Out Trading Card Game 2004–2005

360 cards. Unnumbered. Svetoslav Todorov. (87 x 61mm). *Complete list can be found on page 197.*

Bulgaria international Svetoslav Todorov, a £750,000 signing from West Ham United in March 2002, scored 26 goals during the 2002/03 title-winning campaign and finished the season as the division's top scorer. A cruciate knee ligament injury sustained during a training match, just before the start of the Premier League campaign, meant he would make only one appearance during the following two seasons.

TOPPS. 2004/05.

Premier Stars

245 cards. *Flix-Pix:* No. 194. Badge, Yakubu and Arjan De Zeeuw (spelt incorrectly on card). (68 x 54mm).

A subset of lenticular cards issued as part of Topps' *Premier Stars* collection. Each card shows the 2003/04 top scorer, Player of the Season and club crest.

No. 204. Amdy Faye. (86 x 60mm). Complete list can be found on page 197.

Senegal international Amdy Faye joined Pompey from French Ligue 1 side AJ Auxerre in August 2003 for £1.5m. The defensive midfielder spent 18 months at Fratton Park, making 52 league and cup appearances, before a £2m move to Newcastle United in January 2005. He went on to have spells at Charlton Athletic, Stoke City and Leeds United.

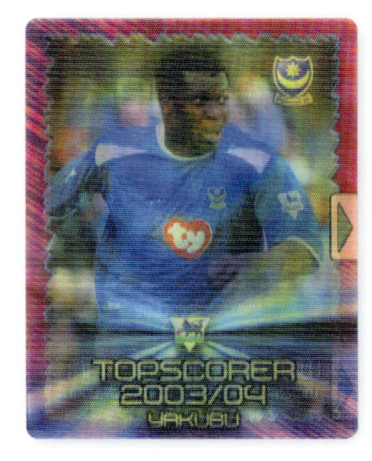

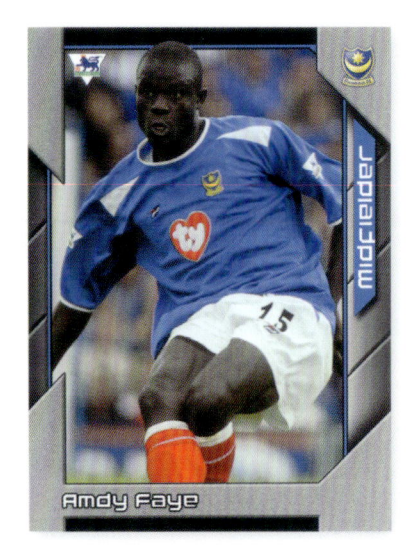

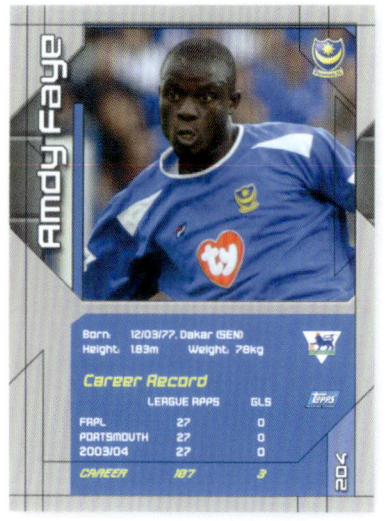

TOPPS/MERLIN. 2004/05.

Kick Off – Season 2004/05 Pocket Collection

382 stickers. No. 308. Yakubu, No. 310. Linvoy Primus, No. 313. Matthew Taylor, No. 322. Alexei Smertin, No. 323. Steve Stone, No. 324. Eyal Berkovic. (59 x 25mm, 30 x 21mm and 30 x 42mm). *Complete list can be found on page 197.*

Attacking midfielder Eyal Berkovic scored three goals in 28 league and cup appearances during the 2004/05 season before sealing a move to his home country with Israeli club Maccabi Tel Aviv.

Subset: Nestlé Smarties Premier League Stars

20 stickers. No. S17. Yakubu. (34 x 34mm).

A subset of 20 circular stickers, issued by Nestlé with packets of Smarties, included striker Yakubu Aiyegbeni who initially joined Pompey on loan from Maccabi Haifa in January 2003. Seven goals in 14 appearances helped clinch the First Division title and earned him a permanent £4m transfer. He finished the 2003/04 season as the club's top scorer with 19 league and cup goals, and scored a total of 43 in 92 matches before moving to Middlesbrough in May 2005. A Nigeria international, Yakubu scored 21 goals in 57 appearances for his country.

TOPPS/MERLIN. 2005/06.

Merlin's Premier Stars

224 cards. No. 159. Sander Westerveld. (85 x 61mm). *Complete list can be found on page 197.*

Ex-Liverpool goalkeeper Sander Westerveld was brought to Pompey by manager Alain Perrin from Real Sociedad on a one-year contract in July 2005. He played only seven games before being loaned to Everton for a month and failed to regain his place upon his return. He was released by the club at the end of the season, joining UD Almería.

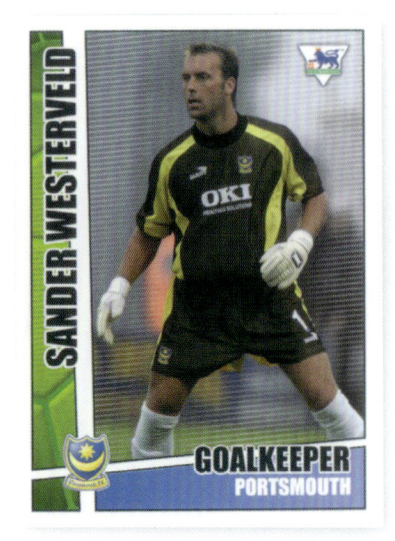

MAGIC BOX INTERNATIONAL. 2005/06.

Shoot Out Trading Card Game 2005–2006

360 cards. Unnumbered. *Update card (60 cards):* Andres D'Alessandro. (87 x 61mm). *Complete list can be found on page 197.*

Argentina international Andres D'Alessandro joined Pompey on loan from Wolfsburg in February 2006 for the remainder of the season. The skilful attacking midfielder's solitary goal for the club was an outstanding effort during a 2-1 defeat to Charlton Athletic at The Valley. Harry Redknapp was keen to sign D'Alessandro on a permanent deal at the end of the season, but he instead opted for a move to Real Zaragoza.

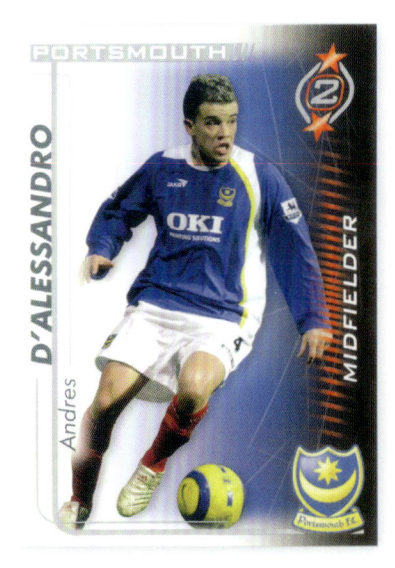

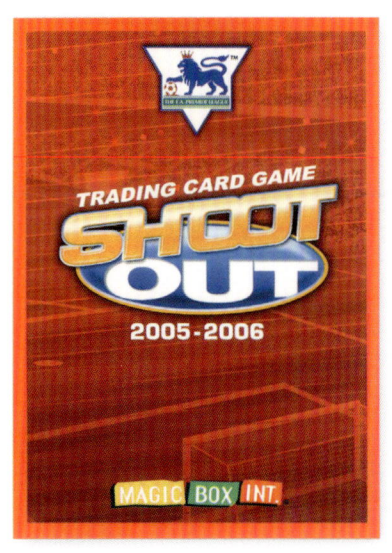

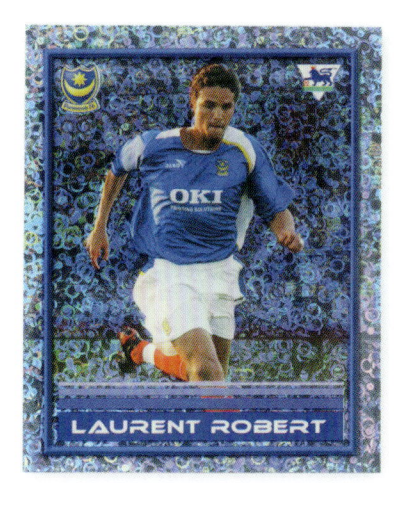

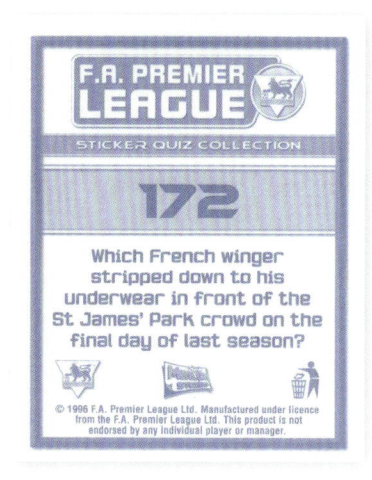

MERLIN. 2005/06.

F.A. Premier League Sticker Quiz Collection

230 stickers. No. 172. Laurent Robert. (68 x 54mm). *Complete list can be found on page 197.*

Laurent Robert spent an unsuccessful spell on loan at Fratton Park between August 2005 and January 2006. The winger scored one goal in 17 league appearances, during a 2-1 defeat away to West Bromwich Albion, before returning to Newcastle United.

MERLIN. 2005/06.

Merlin's F.A. Premier League 06 Official Sticker Collection – Autograph Edition

528 stickers. No. 391. Dario Silva. (68 x 54mm). *Complete list can be found on page 197.*

Dario Silva had spent the majority of his career in Italy and Spain before moving to Pompey from Sevilla in September 2005. The Uruguay international failed to make an impact following an ankle injury and was released from his contract in February 2006 having scored three goals in 15 matches. The following September he was seriously injured in a car crash in Montevideo which resulted in his right leg being amputated below the knee.

PORTSMOUTH F.C. 2005/06.

Junior Blues Club Player Cards

Unknown number in series. Unnumbered. Dejan Stefanovic. (178 x 127mm).

Centre-back Dejan Stefanovic, a £1.85m capture from Vitesse Arnhem in the summer of 2003, was a regular starter during his first two seasons with Pompey. The Serbian's consistent displays were recognised when he was voted the fans' Player of the Season 2004/05 and the following season he was appointed as captain. The 2006/07 season saw him switch to left-back, before the arrival of Hermann Hreidarsson and Sylvain Distin threatened his place in the side and he moved to Fulham in August 2007. A version of this set was also issued without the Junior Blues Club logos.

MAGIC BOX INTERNATIONAL. 2006/07.

Shoot Out Trading Card Game 2006–2007

360 cards. Unnumbered. Kanu. (87 x 61mm). *Complete list can be found on page 198.*

Nwankwo Kanu joined Pompey on a free transfer from West Bromwich Albion in the summer of 2006. The former Ajax, Inter Milan and Arsenal striker played 167 games, scoring 28 goals. He finished his first season at Fratton Park as top scorer and scored the winning goal in both the 2008 FA Cup Semi-Final and Final.

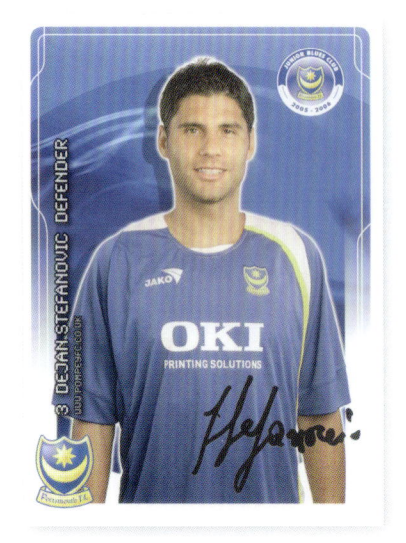

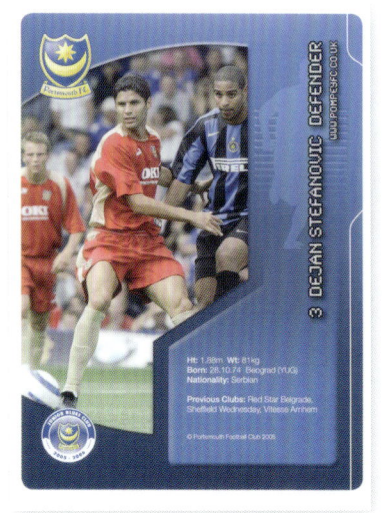

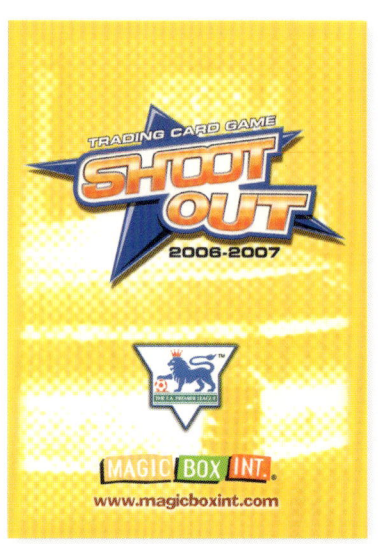

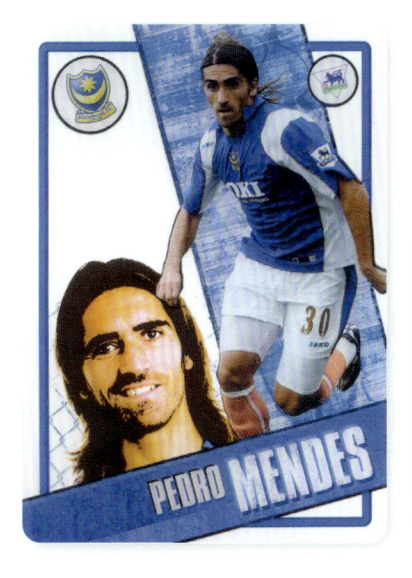

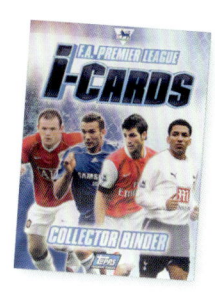

TOPPS. 2006/07.
F.A. Premier League i-Cards

100 clear plastic cards. No. 66. Glen Johnson, No. 67. Sol Campbell, No. 68. Sean Davis, No. 69. Pedro Mendes, No. 70. Kanu. (89 x 64mm).

Portugal international Pedro Mendes joined Pompey from Tottenham Hotspur as part of a combined deal with Sean Davis and Noe Pamarot for £7.5m in January 2006. His first two goals were both memorable 25-yard strikes in a vital win against Manchester City at Fratton Park two months later. He won the FA Cup with Pompey in 2008 before moving to Rangers having made 68 appearances, scoring five goals.

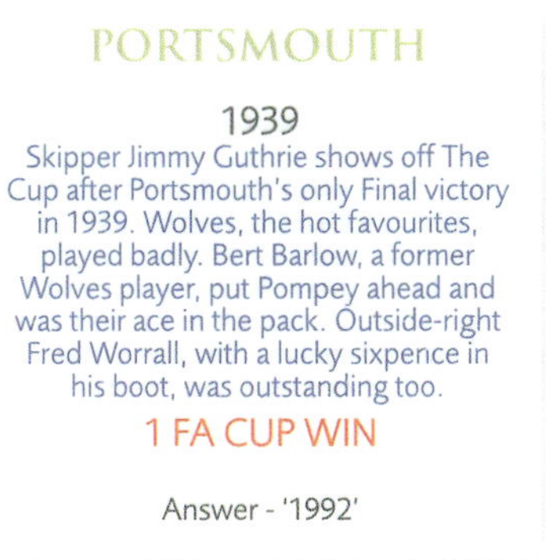

TEXACO. 2007.
The FA Cup Winners Hall of Fame

24 tiles. Unnumbered. Portsmouth. (50 x 50mm).

In 2007 Texaco gave away plastic tiles, featuring each of the 24 FA Cup-winning clubs, with every £10 of fuel purchased.

PORTSMOUTH
1939

Skipper Jimmy Guthrie shows off The Cup after Portsmouth's only Final victory in 1939. Wolves, the hot favourites, played badly. Bert Barlow, a former Wolves player, put Pompey ahead and was their ace in the pack. Outside-right Fred Worrall, with a lucky sixpence in his boot, was outstanding too.

1 FA CUP WIN

Answer – '1992'

TOPPS. 2007.

Premier Gold

170 cards. *Star Player*: No. R14. Sol Campbell. (89 x 64mm). *Complete list can be found on page 198.*

England international Sol Campbell signed a two-year deal with Pompey in August 2006, joining from Arsenal on a free transfer. During his three-year stay he lifted the FA Cup as captain in 2008 and helped his side avoid relegation in 2008/09. Campbell left the club in September 2009 having played 111 games, scoring two goals.

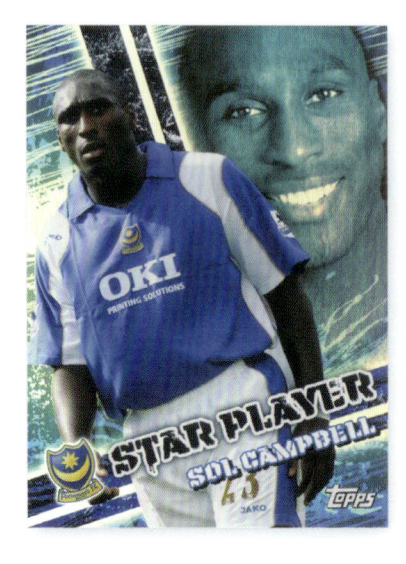

MERLIN. 2006/07.

Merlin's Kick Off F.A. Premier League Sticker Collection

201 stickers. No. 137. Benjamin Mwaruwari. (68 x 54mm). *Complete list can be found on page 198.*

Benjani Mwaruwari had two spells with Pompey between 2006 and 2012. The Zimbabwe international signed from Auxerre for £4.1m in January 2006 and his first goal, scored at Wigan Athletic, helped keep relegation-threatened Pompey in the Premier League. A return of six goals, then a further 12 in the first half of the 2007/08 season earned him a move to Manchester City. He returned to Fratton Park in August 2011, but struggled to rediscover the form that had endeared him to Pompey's fans. Benjani made a total of 94 league and cup appearances, scoring 20 goals.

MERLIN. 2006/07.

Merlin's F.A. Premier League 07 Official Sticker Collection

522 stickers. No. 356. Johnson. (68 x 54mm). *Complete list can be found on page 198.*

Glen Johnson made 100 appearances, scoring four goals, between 2006 and 2009. An England international, he joined on a season-long loan from Chelsea ahead of signing a four-year contract in the summer of 2007. He was the first-choice right-back, and played in the 2008 FA Cup Final before transferring to Liverpool for £17.5m.

MATCH!. 2007.

Super Striker Game Cards!

36 cards. Unnumbered. Kanu, Lomana LuaLua. (70 x 68mm).

A Top Trumps-style game, issued as four sheets of nine perforated cards, included with the first issue of Match! Collectors' Special! magazine.

Congolese striker Lomana LuaLua joined on loan from Newcastle United in February 2004. Several impressive performances, and four goals in 15 games, secured him a permanent deal at the end of the season. Well-known for his acrobatic goal celebrations, his most memorable strikes were a brace against Southampton in a 4-1 Fratton Park victory in April 2005. LuaLua joined Olympiacos in August 2007 having scored 19 goals in 91 appearances.

THE POMPEY STUDY CENTRE. 2006/07.

Pompey Trumps

30 cards. Unnumbered. Jack Tinn. (88 x 62mm). *Complete list can be found on page 198.*

The Pompey Study Centre provided packs of *Pompey Trumps* cards to children during the 2006/07 and 2007/08 seasons to promote healthy eating as part of the Kick Start Health initiative.

Jack Tinn began his managerial career with South Shields before taking charge at Pompey in 1927. He led the club to three FA Cup Finals and famously wore a pair of 'lucky' spats over his shoes throughout the cup run to the 1939 final.

THE POMPEY STUDY CENTRE. 2007/08.

Pompey Trumps

30 cards. Unnumbered. Hermann Hreidarsson. (88 x 62mm). *Complete list can be found on page 198.*

Hermann Hreidarsson joined on a free transfer from Charlton Athletic in August 2007 and enjoyed a successful maiden season at Fratton Park. The left-back scored his first goal during the 7-4 win against Reading in September and was a member of the FA Cup-winning side. He played a total of 123 games, scoring eight goals, before moving to Coventry City in January 2012. An Iceland international, Hreidarsson made 89 appearances for his country.

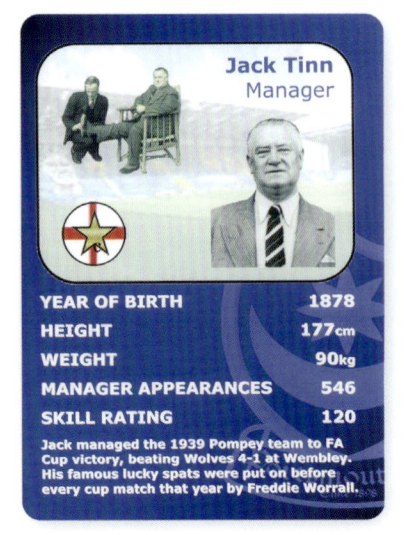

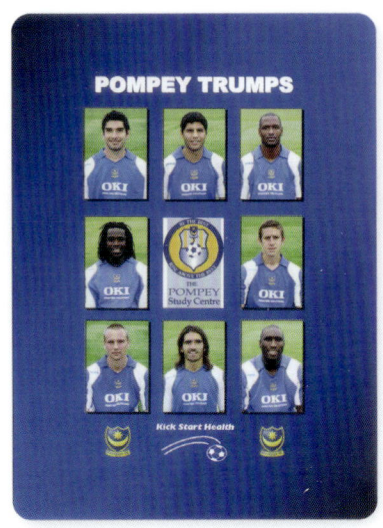

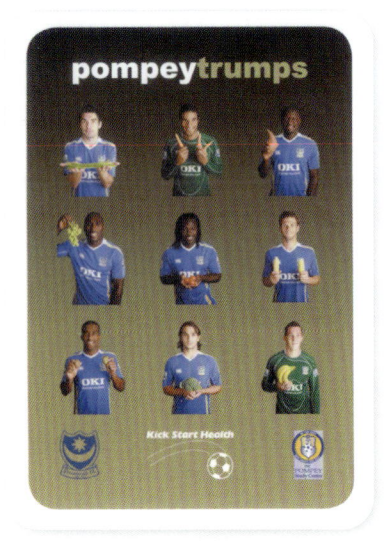

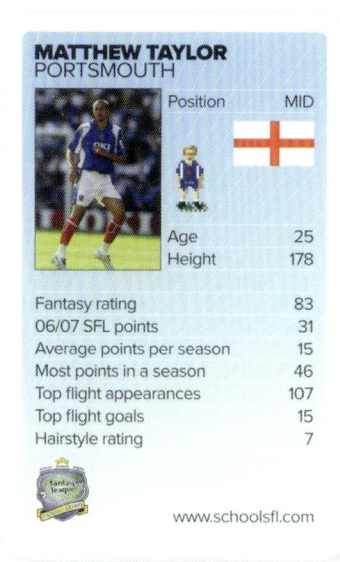

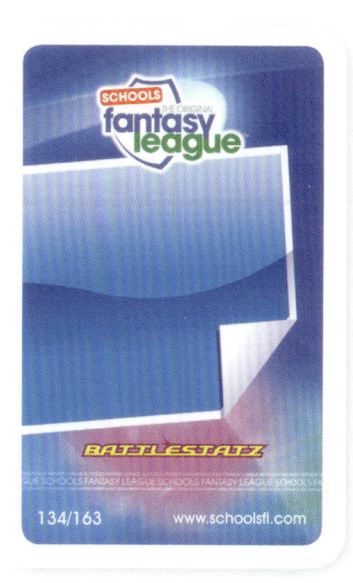

SCHOOLS FANTASY LEAGUE. 2007/08.

Player Cards

131 cards. No. 10. David James, No. 46. Sol Campbell, No. 47. Sylvain Distin, No. 77. Matthew Taylor. (86 x 56mm).

Schools Fantasy League cards were given to Year 6 children at participating schools during the 2007/08 and 2009/10 seasons and could be used to play a Top Trumps-style game.

Matt Taylor joined from Luton Town in July 2002 and was a regular at left wing-back in the 2002/03 First Division title-winning side. He scored the winning penalty in the vital 2-1 victory at Wigan Athletic in April 2006 which kept the club in the Premier League. Taylor joined Bolton Wanderers in January 2008 having made 203 appearances, scoring 29 goals.

SCHOOLS FANTASY LEAGUE. 2009/10.

Battlestatz

163 cards. No. 12. David James, No. 101. Niko Kranjcar, No. 134. David Nugent. (86 x 56mm).

A £6m signing from Preston North End in July 2007, David Nugent appeared as a substitute in the 2008 FA Cup Final, replacing John Utaka in the 69th minute. He finished the 2010/11 season as the club's top scorer with 14 goals before a summer switch to Leicester City. Nugent made a total of 93 appearances for Pompey, scoring 20 goals.

MERLIN. 2007/08.

Merlin's Premier League 2008 Sticker Collection

648 stickers. No. 478. Linvoy Primus. (68 x 54mm). *Complete list can be found on page 198.*

Linvoy Primus joined on a free transfer from Reading in 2000. The defender suffered numerous injury setbacks during his first two seasons at Fratton Park and struggled to break into the first team. The 2002/03 championship-winning season saw Primus seize his opportunity, however, and he was voted both the Fans' and PFA Fans' Player of the Year. In 2015 he was awarded an MBE in recognition of his charity work with Faith and Football, which he set up in 2002.

MERLIN. 2007/08.

Merlin's Kick Off Season 2007/08 Sticker Collection

230 stickers. No. 172. Gary O'Neil. (68 x 54mm). *Complete list can be found on page 198.*

Midfielder Gary O'Neil came through the youth ranks at Fratton Park, making his senior debut aged 16 versus Barnsley in January 2000. A member of the squad promoted to the Premier League in 2003, and the side that narrowly avoided relegation in 2006, he moved to Middlesbrough in August 2007 for £5m having made 192 appearances.

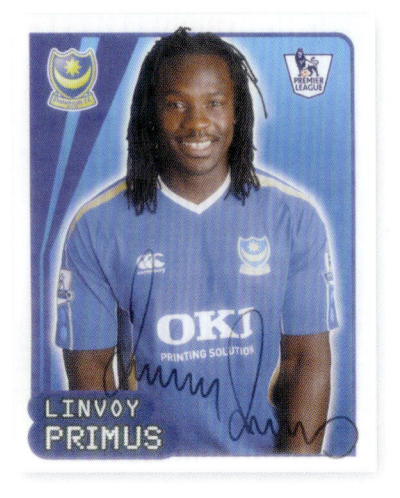

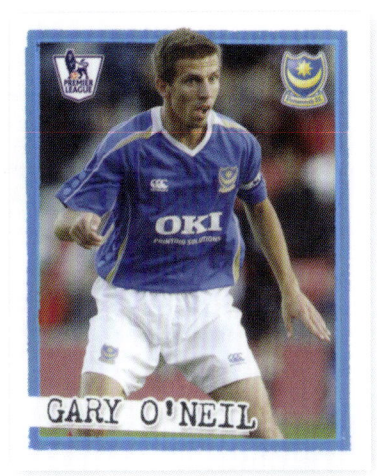

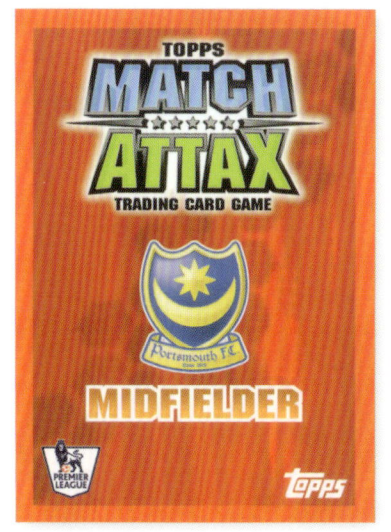

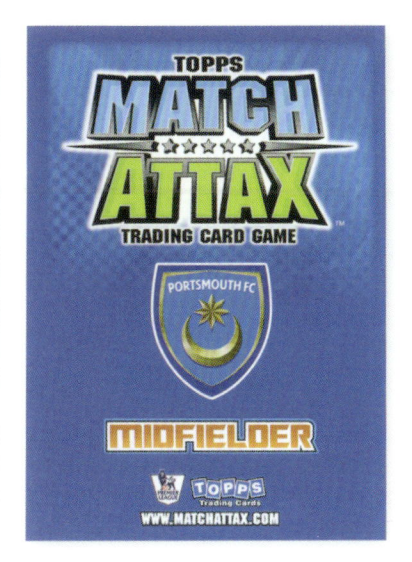

TOPPS. 2007/08.
Match Attax Trading Card Game

562 cards. Unnumbered. *Base Set:* Niko Kranjcar. (87 x 62mm). *Complete list can be found on page 199.*

The 2007/08 season saw the release of the first Topps *Match Attax Trading Card Game* collection. Croatia international Niko Kranjcar played 100 games for Pompey, scoring 12 goals, between August 2006 and September 2009. The attacking midfielder began his career at Dinamo Zagreb then had a spell with Hajduk Split before moving to Fratton Park for £3.5m having impressed at the 2006 World Cup in Germany.

TOPPS. 2008/09.
Match Attax Trading Card Game

447 cards. Unnumbered. *Base Set:* Lassana Diarra. (87 x 62mm). *Complete list can be found on page 199.*

Defensive midfielder Lassana Diarra joined Pompey from Arsenal in January 2008 for £5m. The France international scored his first goal for the club during the FA Cup Fourth Round tie against Plymouth Argyle at Fratton Park, and played in all the remaining rounds on the way to the final. In September 2008 he scored Pompey's first goal in a major European competition versus Vitoria de Guimaraes in the UEFA Cup, before moving to Real Madrid the following January for £18.8m.

TOPPS. 2008/09.

Total Football 2009 Premier League Sticker Collection

480 stickers. No. 352. Peter Crouch. (68 x 54mm). *Complete list can be found on page 199.*

England international striker Peter Crouch first joined Pompey in 2001 from Queens Park Rangers in a deal worth £1.5m. His time at Fratton Park was cut short, however, when 19 goals in 39 appearances persuaded Aston Villa to part with £5m for his services in March 2002. Spells with Southampton and Liverpool followed before he rejoined Pompey in July 2008 for £11m. He scored 16 goals in 49 appearances in 2008/09, including four during the UEFA Cup campaign, before transferring to Tottenham Hotspur in July 2009.

MATCH!. 2008/09.

Quiz Cards

24 cards. Unnumbered. Jermain Defoe. (85 x 55mm).

Striker Jermain Defoe signed from Tottenham Hotspur for £7.5m in January 2008, scoring eight goals in his first seven games, including an equaliser in a 1-1 draw against Chelsea on his debut. The England international hit 17 goals in 36 appearances before moving back to Spurs for £15.75m in January 2009.

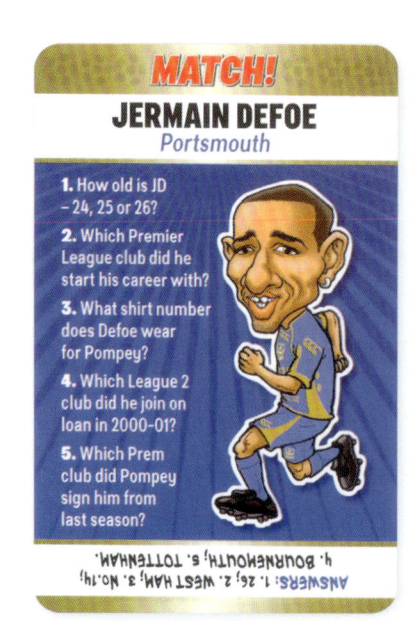

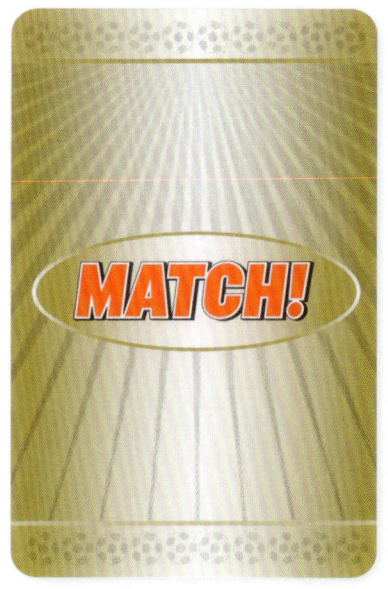

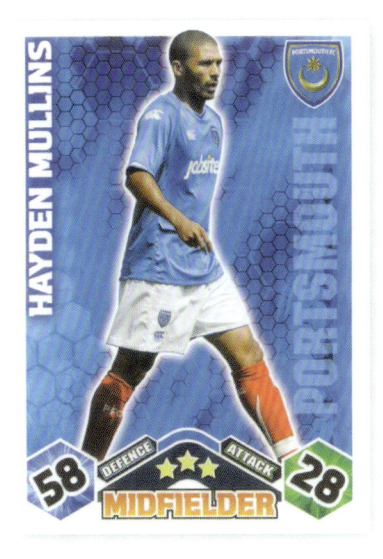

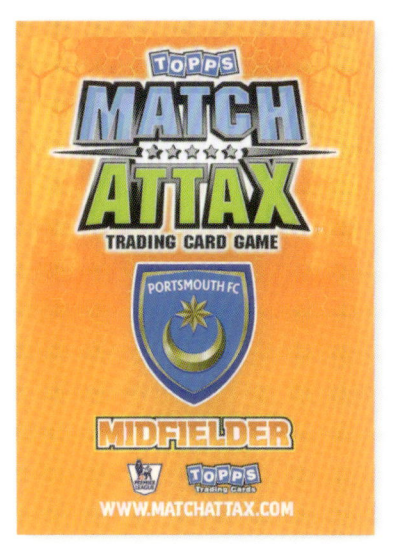

TOPPS. 2009/10.
Match Attax Trading Card Game

455 cards. Unnumbered. Base Set: Hayden Mullins. (87 x 62mm). *Complete list can be found on page 199.*

Hayden Mullins spent the first ten years of his career with Crystal Palace and West Ham United before manager Tony Adams brought him to Pompey on a three-and-a-half-year deal in January 2009. He played in the 2010 FA Cup Final, and was voted Player of the Season the following year. Towards the end of the 2011/12 season he joined Reading on loan, before moving to Birmingham City, having made 128 appearances for Pompey, scoring three goals.

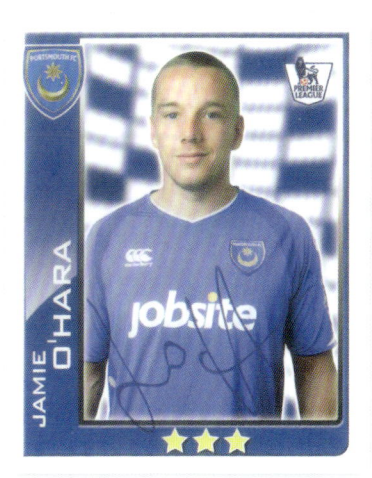

TOPPS. 2009/10.
Topps Premier League Official 2010 Sticker Collection

462 stickers. No. 326. Jamie O'Hara. (68 x 54mm). *Complete list can be found on page 199.*

Jamie O'Hara had an eventful loan spell with Pompey between September 2009 and May 2010. Within the space of nine months he had played in the FA Cup Final defeat to Chelsea, suffered relegation, and been voted Pompey's Player of the Season. O'Hara returned to Tottenham Hotspur, his parent club, at the end of the season.

THE PST AND THE TORNANTE COMPANY

In March 2010 debt-ridden Pompey, by now under the control of their fourth owner of the season, became the first Premier League club to be placed into administration. The resulting nine-point deduction left them 17 points adrift at the bottom of the table and by April relegation was confirmed. The solitary highlight during a miserable season was the FA Cup run which led to a second final appearance in two years that ended in a 1-0 defeat at the hands of Chelsea.

In February 2012 the club entered administration for a second time and by the time the Pompey Supporters' Trust (PST) had wrestled the club from reluctant owner Balram Chainrai 14 months later, Pompey had suffered a third relegation in four seasons. However, just 18 months later, the PST declared the club debt-free and in May 2017 Pompey secured promotion back to League One under manager Paul Cook. The following August, The Tornante Company, headed by the former Disney CEO Michael Eisner, completed a takeover after their offer for the club was accepted by community shareholders a couple of months beforehand. Kenny Jackett was appointed as manager in June 2017 following Cook's departure to Wigan Athletic. Following a 5-4 penalty shoot-out win versus Sunderland in the Checkatrade Trophy Final, he guided Pompey to two play-off semi-finals in 2019 and 2020 which both ended in defeat to Sunderland and Oxford United respectively. Pompey spent Christmas 2021 at the top of the table, but by mid-March they had dropped out of the play-off places. Five consecutive defeats, including the delayed 2020 Papa John's Trophy Final versus Salford City after a penalty shoot-out, resulted in Jackett leaving the club.

Danny Cowley was installed as head coach, assisted by brother Nicky, until the end of the season. Their first full season in charge concluded with a 10th-place finish in 2021/22. After a bright start to the 2022/23 season, a run of nine league games without a win saw the Cowleys sacked following a 3-1 home defeat to Charlton Athletic on New Year's Day. Simon Bassey was installed as interim head coach ahead of the appointment of John Mousinho on 20th January 2023.

2011–2022

PANINI. 2010/11.
nPower Championship Official Sticker Collection 2011

386 stickers. *International:* No. 289. Liam Lawrence. (68 x 54mm). *Complete list can be found on page 199.*

Liam Lawrence arrived at Pompey on the eve of the 2010/11 season from Stoke City as part of an exchange deal, along with Dave Kitson, which saw Marc Wilson move to the Britannia Stadium. The Republic of Ireland international exited Fratton Park in August 2012 with the club in administration.

TOPPS. 2011/12.
Match Attax Trading Card Game Championship Edition

293 cards. Unnumbered. *Base Set:* David Norris. (87 x 62mm). *Complete list can be found on page 199.*

Midfielder David Norris signed on a free-transfer from Ipswich Town in June 2011. He played 42 matches, scoring eight goals, including a memorable 93rd-minute equaliser in the 2-2 draw with Southampton at St Mary's Stadium in April 2012. He joined Leeds United just over a year after his arrival.

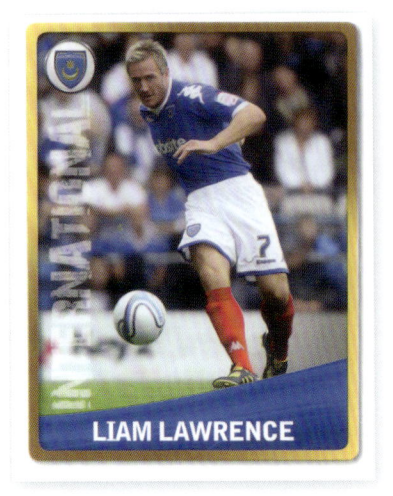

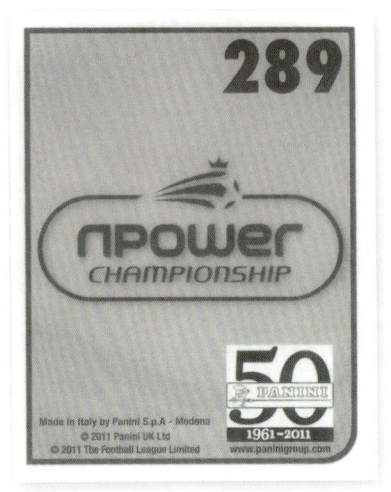

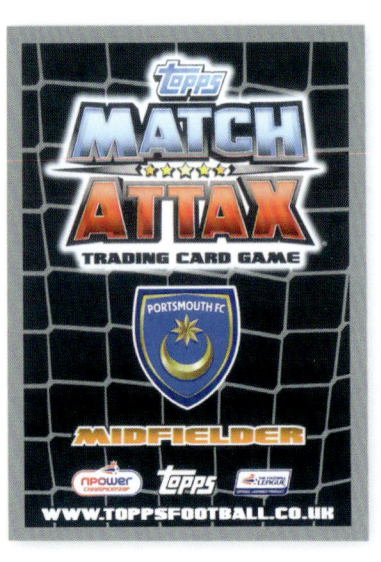

Collectible cards featuring both past and current players were issued with the Official Programme during the 2011/12 and 2013/14 seasons.

PORTSMOUTH F.C. OFFICIAL PROGRAMME. 2011/12.

Fratton Heroes

80 cards. No. 64. Ray Hiron. (118 x 80mm).

Gosport-born striker Ray Hiron was spotted by Pompey scouts playing for Fareham Town in 1964 and signed terms during his lunch break while working at Portsmouth Dockyard. He scored 119 goals in 373 matches during his 11 years at Fratton Park.

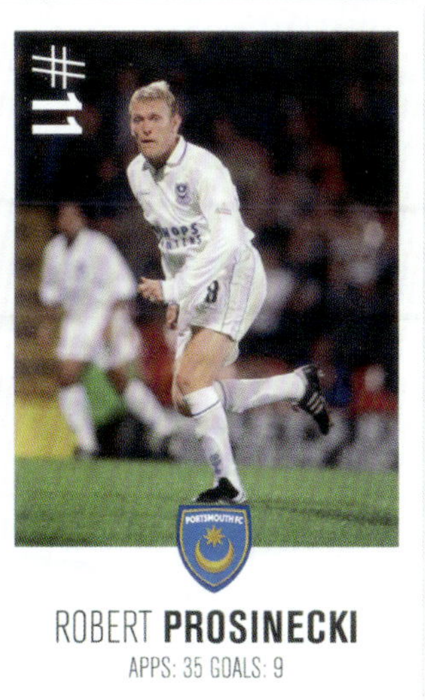

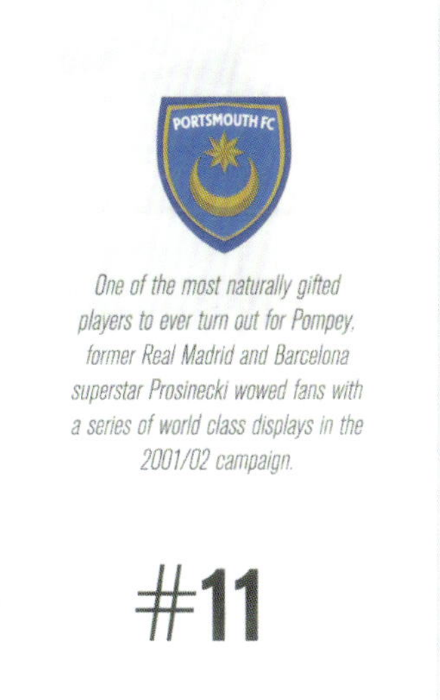

PORTSMOUTH F.C. OFFICIAL PROGRAMME. 2013/14.

Player Cards

100 cards. No. 11. Robert Prosinecki. (122 x 76mm).

Robert Prosinecki signed a one-year contract in the summer of 2001, with chairman Milan Mandaric describing his arrival as "a present to the fans". The supremely talented midfielder had won a European Cup, played in four major international tournaments and had spells with Barcelona and Real Madrid before arriving at Pompey. In 2008, Prosinecki was selected by readers of The News as part of an all-time greatest Portsmouth XI.

TOPPS. 2015/16.

*Premier Gold
(All-Time Accolades subset)*

20 cards. No. AA-8. David James. Base card shown below. *Parallel cards:* purple #/50, black #/25, orange #/11, premier gold 1/1. (62 x 87mm). *Oversize limited edition:* #/199. (126 x 178mm).

England goalkeeper David James made 158 appearances for Pompey between August 2006 and May 2010. He kept a clean sheet during the 2008 FA Cup win and captained the side for the 2010 final, his last game for the club. James left Pompey at the end of the 2009/10 season and played for Bristol City and Bournemouth before joining manager Hermann Hreidarsson at Icelandic side IBV Vestmannaeyjar as player-coach.

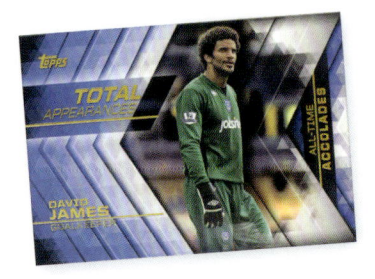

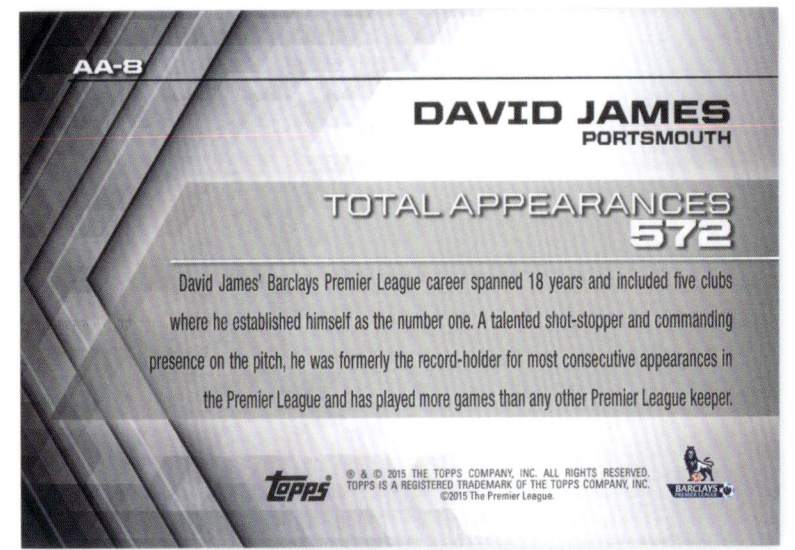

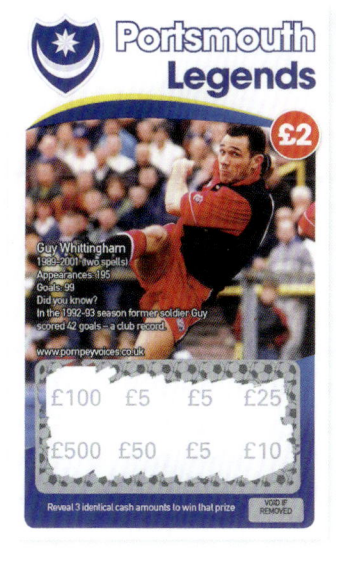

POMPEY DEVELOPMENT ASSOCIATION. 2016/17.

Portsmouth Legends

10 scratchcards. Unnumbered. Bert Barlow, Jimmy Dickinson, Johnny Gordon, Peter Harris, Billy Haines, Kanu, Alan Knight, A.E. Knight, Len Phillips, Guy Whittingham. (140 x 82mm).

A series of ten *Portsmouth Legends* scratchcards, sold on match days during the 2016/17 season.

TOPPS/PORTSMOUTH FC. 2017.

Portsmouth FC
2016/17 Trading Cards

27 cards. Unnumbered. Paul Cook, Christian Burgess. (87 x 62mm).
Complete list can be found on page 200.

Topps, at the time part-owned by The Tornante Company, issued a limited edition pack of trading cards, featuring the squad which won the League Two title, with Junior Blues membership packs during the 2017/18 season.

Paul Cook was appointed manager in May 2015 and led Pompey to the League Two title two years later before taking charge at Wigan Athletic.

Centre-back Christian Burgess was one of Paul Cook's first signings during the summer of 2015. He spent five seasons at Fratton Park before joining Belgian club Union SG in July 2020 having made 210 appearances.

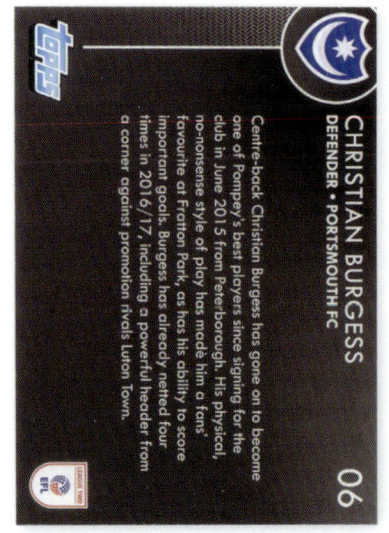

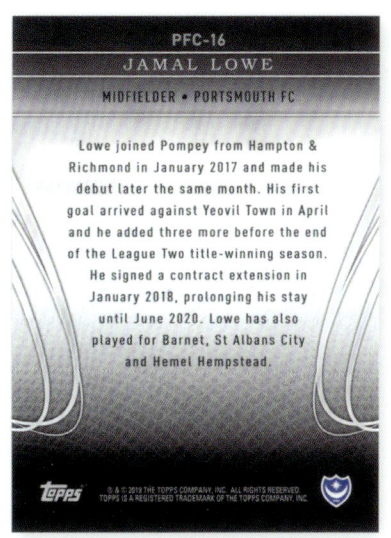

TOPPS/PORTSMOUTH FC. 2019.

*Portsmouth FC
2019 Collector Cards*

30 cards (signed and unsigned). No. 16. Jamal Lowe, No. 28. Brett Pitman. (89 x 63mm). *Complete list can be found on page 200.*

Available as a limited edition pack pre-signed with authentic player autographs, or with one signed card per set. Each pack contained a poster showcasing the collection.

Jamal Lowe joined Pompey from Hampton & Richmond Borough in January 2017. The winger scored two goals in the 3-1 victory at Notts County the following April which secured promotion to League One. Lowe hit Pompey's equaliser in the Checkatrade Trophy Final before transferring to Wigan Athletic in August 2019.

Striker Brett Pitman spent three seasons at Fratton Park after joining from Ipswich Town in 2017. He scored 41 goals in 99 appearances before a move to Swindon Town in September 2020.

TOPPS/PORTSMOUTH FC. 2019.

Portsmouth FC Checkatrade Trophy Winners 2019. Shirt cards and Shirt/Autograph cards

14 cards (signed and unsigned). #/180. No. 1. Craig MacGillivray, No. 13. Gareth Evans. (62 x 87mm). Complete list can be found on page 200.

Following the 2019 Checkatrade Trophy Final versus Sunderland at Wembley, Topps issued a limited edition collection of cards featuring sections of the shirts worn by the players during the match. Signed and unsigned varieties were issued, limited to 180 of each, with complete sets limited to 30 packs.

Goalkeeper Craig MacGillivray arrived from Shrewsbury Town in the summer of 2018, signing a two-year deal. He made a crucial save in the Checkatrade Trophy Final penalty shoot-out which Pompey won 5-4 after the game had finished 2-2 following extra-time. MacGillivray joined Charlton Athletic in June 2021 following 135 appearances.

Gareth Evans joined Pompey on a free-transfer from Fleetwood Town and was a key member of the side which won the League Two championship in 2016/17. The midfielder transferred to Bradford City in September 2020 having made 218 appearances, scoring 38 goals, during a five-year spell at Fratton Park.

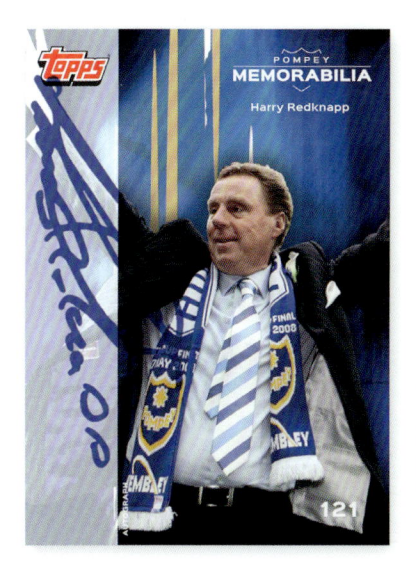

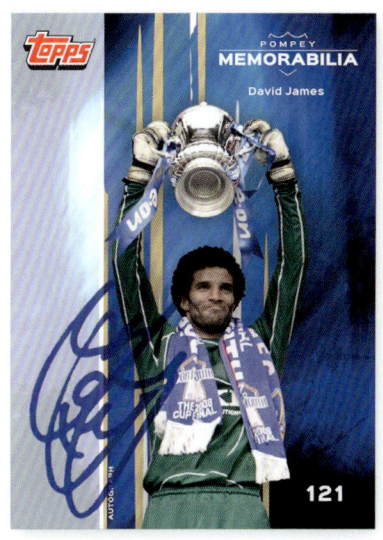

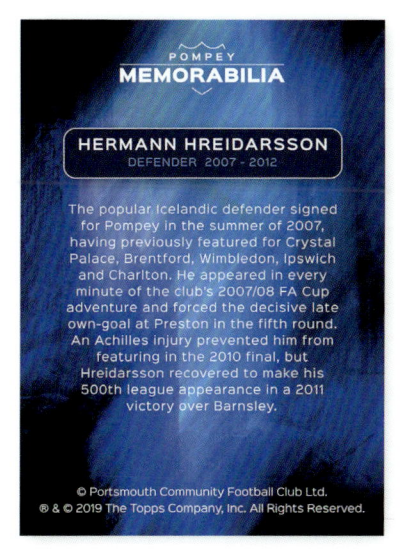

TOPPS/PORTSMOUTH FC. 2019.

2008 FA Cup Winners Limited Edition Collectors Box Set

3 cards. #/200. Harry Redknapp, David James, Herman Hreidarsson. (89 x 63mm).

Portsmouth Football Club collaborated with Topps to produce a limited edition box set commemorating Pompey's famous 2008 FA Cup Final victory.

Limited to 200 sets, each box contains three personally hand-signed and individually numbered collector cards, replica FA Cup winners' medal and a seven-inch high-definition screen pre-loaded with highlights from Pompey's FA Cup-winning run.

2011–2022 | 191

TOPPS/PORTSMOUTH FC. 2020.

Portsmouth FC 2019/20 Collector Cards

29 cards (signed and unsigned). Unnumbered. Tom Naylor, Ronan Curtis. *New Signings Booster Pack:* Cameron McGeehan. (90 x 65mm). Complete list can be found on page 200.

Signed and unsigned packs of this set were available to purchase. The signed set was limited to 250 boxes. A booster pack of three cards featuring new signings was added towards the end of the season. Each set included a poster showcasing the collection.

Midfielder and captain Tom Naylor won consecutive promotions with Burton Albion before arriving at Fratton Park in June 2018. He joined Wigan Athletic when his deal expired in June 2021.

Ronan Curtis signed from Derry City in the summer of 2018. The Republic of Ireland forward scored 12 goals in his first season on the south coast.

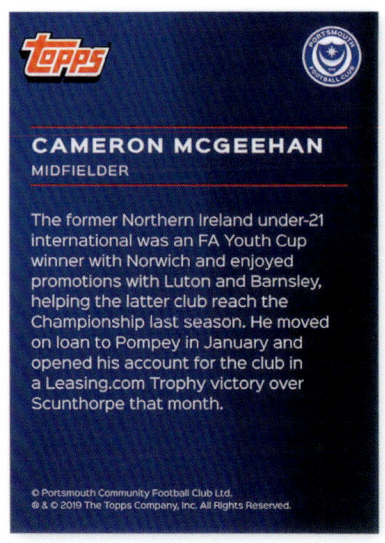

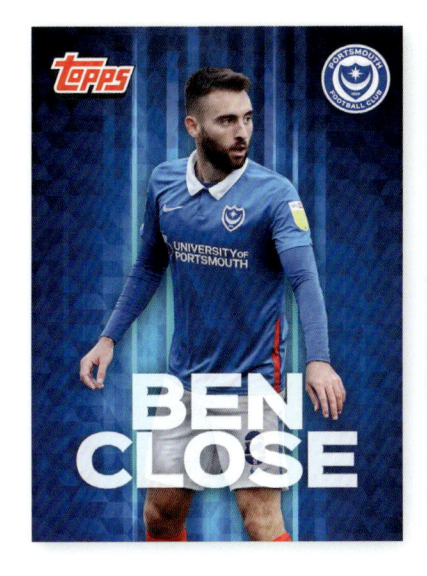

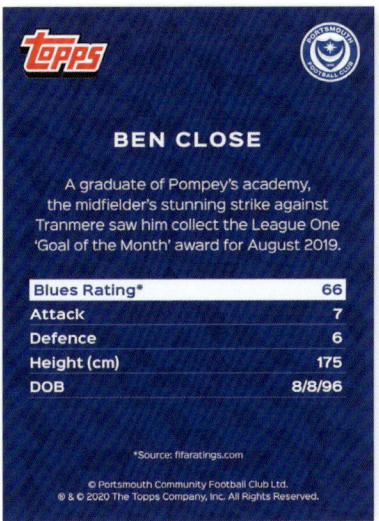

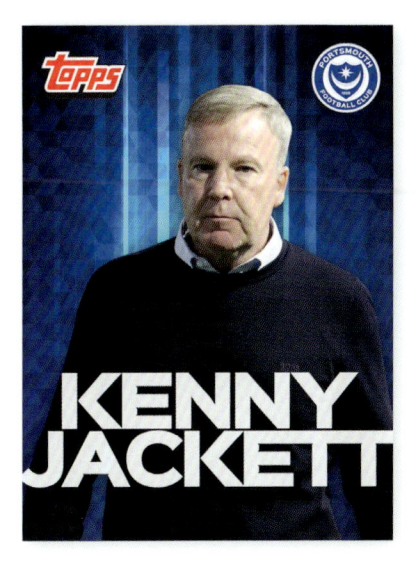

TOPPS/PORTSMOUTH FC. 2021.

Portsmouth FC 2020/21 Collector Cards

30 cards (signed and unsigned). Unnumbered. Ben Close. (90 x 65mm). *Complete list can be found on page 200.*

Available as both signed and unsigned sets, the 2020/21 player cards featured Attack and Defence statistics, plus an overall Blues Rating. A booster pack of Danny and Nicky Cowley cards was released following their appointment.

Portsmouth-born midfielder Ben Close spent his youth in Pompey's academy and signed a professional contract in 2014. A Pompey supporter, he made 190 appearances, scoring 18 goals, before joining Doncaster Rovers in June 2021.

Kenny Jackett took charge at Fratton Park in the summer of 2017, leading Pompey to two League One play-off semi-finals and two EFL Trophy finals, before leaving the club in March 2021.

Winger Michael Jacobs joined Pompey in September 2020 having left Wigan Athletic at the end of the 2019/20 season.

TOPPS/PORTSMOUTH FC. 2021/22.

2021/22 Portsmouth FC – Topps Now

19 base cards. No. 001. Connor Ogilvie – 11.12.2021– print run: 73, No. 002. Gavin Bazunu – 01.01.2022 – print run: 406, No. 005. Denver Hume – 31.01.2022 – print run: 49, No. 007. Aiden O'Brien – 26.02.2022 – print run: 60, No. 009. Sean Raggett – 05.03.2022 – print run: 11. (63 x 89mm and 89 x 63mm). *Complete list can be found on page 200.*

In December 2021, Portsmouth FC teamed up with Topps to release the first in a series of print on demand *Topps Now* cards, featuring the biggest moments, goals and milestones of the season.

Connor Ogilvie signed for Pompey on a free transfer from Gillingham ahead of the 2021/22 campaign. This card commemorates the versatile defender's first goal for the club in the 2-0 victory against Morecambe on 11th December 2021 at Fratton Park.

Republic of Ireland goalkeeper Gavin Bazunu joined Pompey on loan from Manchester City for the 2021/22 season. He made his name on the international stage saving a Cristiano Ronaldo penalty during a World Cup qualifying match versus Portugal in September 2021. Bazunu made 46 appearances, keeping 17 clean sheets, and his outstanding contribution was recognised when he was voted Players' Player of the Season at the club's awards dinner.

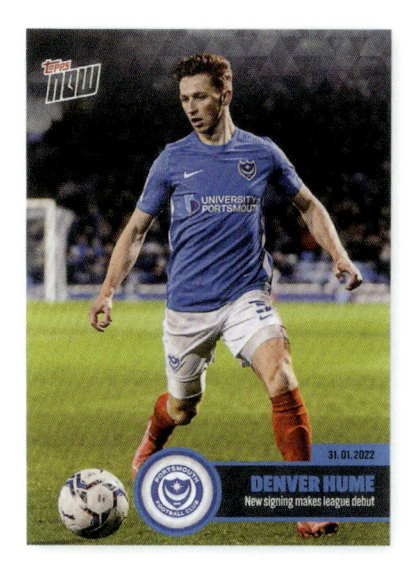

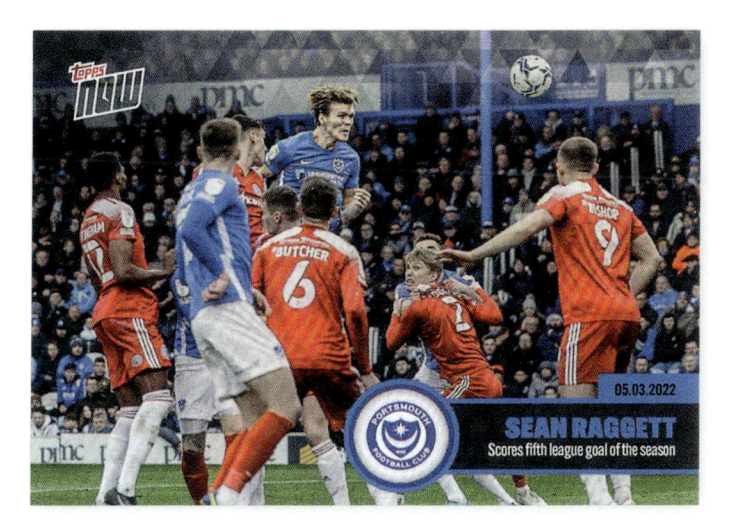

Denver Hume joined Pompey from Sunderland where he started his career, signing a two-and-a-half-year contract. The left-sided defender made his league debut in the 2-1 home defeat to Charlton Athletic on 31st January 2022.

Forward Aiden O'Brien arrived on loan from Sunderland on deadline day in January 2022. He scored five goals in 17 appearances, including a third goal in three games as Pompey came back from three goals down to salvage a point against Fleetwood Town at Fratton Park.

Sean Raggett scored a famous 89th-minute winner for Lincoln City in the 2016/17 FA Cup Fifth Round at Premier League Burnley to send Danny Cowley's National League side through to the quarter-finals. The centre-back switched to Norwich City in 2017 before joining Pompey on loan in June 2019, and signed a permanent deal in August 2020. Raggett is pictured scoring his fifth league goal of the season during a 4-0 home win versus Accrington Stanley.

COMPLETE CARDS AND STICKERS LISTS

PANINI. 1987/88.
Football 88

574 stickers. No. 213. Badge, No. 214. Noel Blake, No. 215. Billy Gilbert, No. 216. Paul Hardyman, No. 217. Clive Whitehead, No. 218. Kevin Dillon, No. 219. Vince Hilaire, No. 220. Alan Ball, No. 221. Alan Knight, No. 222. Team, No. 223. Mick Kennedy, No. 224. Mike Fillery, No. 225. Mike Quinn, No. 226. Ian Baird, No. 227. Ian Stewart, No. 228. Terry Connor.

DAILY MIRROR. 1987/88.
Soccer 88

360 stickers. No. 183. Alan Ball, No. 184. Kenny Swain, No. 185. Alan Knight, No. 186. Noel Blake, No. 187. Vince Hilaire, No. 188. Mick Quinn, No. 189. Micky Fillery, No. 190. Paul Mariner, No. 191. Terry Connor, No. 192. Billy Gilbert, No. 193. Ian Baird, No. 194. Kevin Dillon, No. 195. Clive Whitehead, No. 196. Mick Kennedy.

W.R. PRIDDY. 1996.
Footballers 1940s–50s

Footballers: No. 28. John Atyeo, No. 45. Bert Barlow, No. 47. Mike Barnard, No. 52. Tony Barton, No. 94. Gerry Bowler, No. 116. Alan Brown, No. 135. Ernie Butler, No. 142. Jimmy Campbell, No. 148. Brian Carter, No. 151. Tom Casey, No. 153. Sammy Chapman, No. 170. Ike Clarke, No. 192. Ray Crawford, No. 210. Reg Cutler, No. 213. Gordon Dale, No. 224. Lindy Delapenha, No. 228. Jim Dickinson, No. 239. Charlie Dore, No. 243. Derek Dougan, No. 246. Ray Drinkwater, No. 295. Harry Ferrier, No. 305. Reg Flewin, No. 320. Jack Froggatt, No. 322. Marcel Gaillard, No. 344. Johnny Gordon, No. 348. Alex Govan, No. 369. Phil Gunter, No. 392. Harry Harris, No. 395. Peter Harris, No. 408. Basil Hayward, No. 414. Jack Henderson, No. 424. Peter Higham, No. 428. Bill Hindmarsh, No. 450. Ron Howells, No. 486. Albert Juliussen, No. 521. Maurice Leather, No. 534. Mick Lill, No. 552. Jimmy McAlinden, No. 556. Sid McClellan, No. 566. Tom McGhee, No. 603. Jack Mansell, No. 604. Barry Mansell, No. 665. Albert Mundy, No. 672. Pat Neil, No. 675. Ron Newman, No. 703. Cliff Parker, No. 719. Harry Penk, No. 723. John Phillips, No. 724. Len Phillips, No. 726. Reg Pickett, No. 728. Ted Platt, No. 730. Ray Pointer, No. 731. Ray Potter, No. 749. Derek Rees, No. 750. Duggie Reid, No. 771. Bill Rochford, No. 773. Phil Rookes, No. 783. Cyril Rutter, No. 785. Terry Ryder, No. 789. Ron Saunders, No. 797. Jimmy Scoular, No. 833. Brian Snowden, No. 835. Jim Spence, No. 848. Jimmy Stephen, No. 861. Jim Strong, No. 888. Bill Thompson, No. 898. Ron Tindall, No. 911. Norman Uprichard, No. 913. Charlie Vaughan, No. 923. Harry Walker, No. 945. Derek Weddle, No. 973. Alex Wilson, No. 997. Jasper Yeuell. *International Squads:* No. 1003. Jimmy Dickinson, No. 1007. Jack Froggatt, No. 1030. Derek Dougan, No. 1042. Norman Uprichard, No. 1045. Allan Brown, No. 1052. Jack Henderson, No. 1060. Jimmy Scoular. *Great Britain:* No. 1092. Jimmy Dickinson.

MERLIN. 2003/04.
F.A. Premier League 2003–2004 Season Pocket Collection

162 stickers. No. 131. Shaka Hislop, No. 132. Hayden Foxe, No. 133. Arjan De Zeeuw, No. 134. Matthew Taylor, No. 135. Nigel Quashie, No. 136. Tim Sherwood, No. 137. Steve Stone, No. 138. Svetoslav Todorov.

MAGIC BOX INTERNATIONAL. 2003/04.
Shoot Out Trading Card Game 2003–2004

360 cards. Unnumbered. Shaka Hislop, Harald Wapenaar, Linvoy Primus, Hayden Foxe, Boris Zivkovic, Arjan De Zeeuw, Dejan Stefanovic, Sebastien Schemmel, Tim Sherwood, Patrik Berger, Nigel Quashie, Steve Stone, Amdy Faye, Alexei Smertin, Svetoslav Todorov, Teddy Sheringham, Yakubu, Vincent Pericard.

TOPPS. 2003/04.
Premier Gold 2004

225 cards. P1. Shaka Hislop, P2. Boris Zivkovic, P3. Steve Stone, P4. Patrik Berger, P5. Teddy Sheringham. *Foil Club Cards:* C17. (Blue and green varieties).

MERLIN. 2003/2004.
Premier League 04

578 stickers. No. 467. Badge, No. 468. Team, *Key Player:* No. 469. Patrik Berger, *Star Striker:* No. 470. Teddy Sheringham,

No. 471. Shaka Hislop, No. 472. Harald Wapenaar, No. 473. Pavel Srnicek, No. 474. Arjan De Zeeuw, No. 475. Hayden Foxe, No. 476. Eddie Howe, No. 477. Linvoy Primus, No. 478. Sebastien Schemmel, No. 479. Dejan Stefanovic, No. 480. Matthew Taylor, No. 481. Boris Zivkovic, No. 482. Patrik Berger, No. 483. Amdy Faye, No. 484. Gary O'Neil, No. 485. Alexei Smertin, No. 486. Nigel Quashie, No. 487. Tim Sherwood, No. 488. Steve Stone, No. 489. Yakubu, No. 490. Vincent Pericard, No. 491. Kevin Harper, No. 492. Teddy Sheringham, No. 493. Svetoslav Todorov, No. 494. Jason Roberts.

MERLIN. 2004/2005.
Premier League 05

574 stickers. No. 463. Badge, No. 464. Squad, No. 465. Home Kit, No. 466. Away Kit, No. 467. Yakubu, No. 468. Arjan De Zeeuw, No. 469. Shaka Hislop, No. 470. Arjan De Zeeuw, No. 471. Andrew Griffin, No. 472. Linvoy Primus, No. 473. Hayden Foxe, No. 474. Dejan Stefanovic, No. 475. Matthew Taylor, No. 476. David Unsworth, No. 477. Nigel Quashie, No. 478. Patrik Berger, No. 479. Eyal Berkovic, No. 480. Aliou Cisse, No. 481. Amdy Faye, No. 482. Steve Stone, No. 483. Svetoslav Todorov, No. 484. Yakubu, No. 485. Ricardo Fuller, No. 486. Lomana LuaLua, No. 487. Harry Redknapp, No. 488. Patrik Berger, No. 489. David Unsworth, No. 490. Ricardo Fuller.

MAGIC BOX INTERNATIONAL. 2004/05.
Shoot Out Trading Card Game 2004–2005

360 cards. Unnumbered. Patrik Berger, Eyal Berkovic, Tom Curtis, Arjan De Zeeuw, Hayden Foxe, Kevin Harper, Shaka Hislop, Lomana LuaLua, Linvoy Primus, Nigel Quashie, Sebastien Schemmel, Dejan Stefanovic, Steve Stone, Matthew Taylor, Svetoslav Todorov, David Unsworth, Harald Wapenaar, Yakubu.

TOPPS. 2004/05.
Premier Stars

245 cards. *Flix-Pix:* No. 194. Badge, Yakubu and Arjan De Zeeuw. No. 195. Shaka Hislop, No. 196. Arjan De Zeeuw, No. 197. Matthew Taylor, No. 198. Dejan Stefanovic, No. 199. David Unsworth, No. 200. Steve Stone, No. 201. Lomana LuaLua, No. 202. Eyal Berkovic, No. 203. Patrik Berger, No. 204. Amdy Faye, No. 205. Yakubu.

TOPPS/MERLIN. 2004/05.
Kick Off Season 2004/05 Pocket Collection

382 stickers. No. 307. Badge, No. 308. Yakubu, No. 309. Shaka Hislop, No. 310. Linvoy Primus, No. 311. Arjan De Zeeuw, No. 312. Dejan Stefanovic, No. 313. Matthew Taylor, No. 314. Steve Stone, No. 315. Eyal Berkovic, No. 316. Alexei Smertin, No. 317. Patrik Berger, No. 318. Yakubu, No. 319. Ivica Mornar, No. 320. Arjan De Zeeuw, No. 321. Dejan Stefanovic, No. 322. Alexei Smertin, No. 323. Steve Stone, No. 324. Eyal Berkovic, No. 325. Patrik Berger.

TOPPS EUROPE/MERLIN COLLECTIONS. 2005/06.
Merlin's Premier Stars

224 cards. No. 159. Sander Westerveld, No. 160. Matthew Taylor, No. 161. Andy O'Brien, No. 162. Dejan Stefanovic, No. 163. Gregory Vignal, No. 164. Andy Griffin, No. 165. Gary O'Neil, No. 166. Giannis Skopelitis, No. 167. Laurent Robert, No. 168. Azar Karadas, No. 169. Lomana LuaLua.

MAGIC BOX INTERNATIONAL. 2005/06.
Shoot Out Trading Card Game 2005–2006

360 cards. Unnumbered. Aliou Cisse, Andy Griffin, Richard Hughes, Azar Karadas, Lomana LuaLua, Ivica Mornar, Andrew O'Brien, Gary O'Neil, Vincent Pericard, Brian Priske, Laurent Robert, Giannis Skopelitis, Dejan Stefanovic, Matthew Taylor, Svetoslav Todorov, John Viafara, Gregory Vignal, Sander Westerveld. *Update cards (60 cards):* Benjani Mwaruwari, Sean Davis, Andres D'Alessandro.

MERLIN. 2005/06.
F.A. Premier League Sticker Quiz Collection

230 stickers. No. 165. Matthew Taylor, No. 166. Andrew O'Brien, No. 167. Lomana LuaLua, No. 168. Ivica Mornar, No. 169. Azar Karadas, No. 170. Gregory Vignal, No. 171. Gary O'Neil, No. 172. Laurent Robert, No. 173. Sander Westerveld, No. 174. Dejan Stefanovic, No. 175. Andrew Griffin.

MERLIN. 2005/06.
F.A. Premier League 06

528 stickers. No. 367. Badge, No. 368. Kit, No. 369. Dejan Stefanovic, No. 370. Team, No. 371. Lomana LuaLua, No. 372. Jamie Ashdown, No. 373. Sander Westerveld, No. 374. Andrew Griffin, No. 375. Andrew O'Brien, No. 376. Linvoy Primus, No. 377. Dejan

Stefanovic, No. 378. Matthew Taylor, No. 379. Gregory Vignal, No. 380. Aliou Cisse, No. 381. Salif Diao, No. 382. Richard Hughes, No. 383. Gary O'Neil, No. 384. Laurent Robert, No. 385. Giannis Skopelitis, No. 386. John Viafara, No. 387. Azar Karadas, No. 388. Lomana LuaLua, No. 389. Collins Mbesuma, No. 390. Ivica Mornar, No. 391. Dario Silva, No. 392. Svetoslav Todorov.

MAGIC BOX INTERNATIONAL. 2006/07.
Shoot Out Trading Card Game 2006-2007

360 cards. Unnumbered. Dean Kiely, David James, Dejan Stefanovic, Glen Johnson, Matthew Taylor, Linvoy Primus, Noe Pamarot, Sol Campbell, Andy O'Brien, Sean Davis, Pedro Mendes, David Thompson, Richard Hughes, Gary O'Neil, Ognjen Koroman, Lomana LuaLua, Benjani Mwaruwari, Kanu. U*pdate Set (72 cards):* Andy Cole, Niko Kranjcar, Lauren, Djimi Traore.

TOPPS. 2007.
Premier Gold

170 cards. No. 100. David James, No. 101. Sol Campbell, No. 102. Glen Johnson, No. 103. Lomana LuaLua, No. 104. Andrew Cole, No. 105. Benjamin Mwaruwari, No. 106. Pedro Mendes. *Star Players:* No. R14. Sol Campbell.

MERLIN. 2006/07.
Kick Off F.A. Premier League Sticker Collection

201 stickers. No. 132. David James, No. 133. Sol Campbell, No. 134. Glen Johnson, No. 135. Lomana LuaLua, No. 136. Matthew Taylor, No. 137. Benjamin Mwaruwari, No. 138. Pedro Mendes, No. 139. Gary O'Neil, No. 140. Sean Davis, No. 141. Svetoslav Todorov.

MERLIN. 2006/07.
F.A. Premier League 07

522 stickers. No. 266. Campbell, No. 348. Badge, No. 349. Team, No. 350. Kit, No. 351. Campbell, No. 352. James, No. 353. Kiely, No. 354. Primus, No. 355. Stefanovic, No. 356. Johnson, No. 357. Campbell, No. 358. O'Brien, No. 359. Pamarot, No. 360. Taylor, No. 361. Fernandes, No. 362. Thompson, No. 363. Koroman, No. 364. Kranjcar, No. 365. Hughes, No. 366. O'Neil, No. 367. Davis, No. 368. Mendes, No. 369. Cole, No. 370. Benjani, No. 371. Kanu, No. 372. LuaLua. *Update sticker:* No. 362. Lauren.

THE POMPEY STUDY CENTRE. 2006/07.
Pompey Trumps

30 cards. Unnumbered. David James, Tony Adams, Linvoy Primus, Dejan Stefanovic, Glen Johnson, Andy O'Brien, Djimi Traore, Andrew Cole, Svetoslav Todorov, Lauren, Noe Pamarot, Matthew Taylor, Jamie Ashdown, Niko Kranjcar, Richard Hughes, Sol Campbell, Benjani, Gary O'Neil, Kanu, Sean Davis, Roudolphe Douala, Pedro Mendes, Lomana LuaLua, Joe Jordan, Guy Whittingham, Jack Tinn, Jimmy Dickinson, Sir Arthur Conan Doyle, Harry Redknapp, Frogmore (Mascot).

THE POMPEY STUDY CENTRE. 2007/08.
Pompey Trumps

30 cards. Unnumbered. David James, Linvoy Primus, Lucien Aubey, Lauren, Glen Johnson, Lassana Diarra, Hermann Hreidarsson, Papa Bouba Diop, Milan Baros, David Nugent, Sulley Muntari, Jermain Defoe, Sylvain Distin, Noe Pamarot, John Utaka, Arnold Mvuemba, Niko Kranjcar, Martin Cranie, Jamie Ashdown, Richard Hughes, Sol Campbell, Richard Duffy, Kanu, Sean Davis, Pedro Mendes, Asmir Begovic, Franck Songo'o, Marc Wilson, Harry Redknapp, Frogmore (Mascot).

MERLIN. 2007/08.
Premier League 2008 Sticker Collection

648 stickers. No. 457. James, No. 458. Johnson, No. 459. Campbell, No. 460. Distin, No. 461. Hreidarsson, No. 462. Kranjcar, No. 463. Davis, No. 464. Bouba Diop, No. 465. Muntari, No. 466. Mwaruwari, No. 467. Utaka, No. 468. Badge, No. 469. Team, No. 470. Home Kit, No. 471. James, No. 472. Johnson, No. 473. Hreidarsson, No. 474. Lauren, No. 475. Pamarot, No. 476. Campbell, No. 477. Distin, No. 478. Primus, No. 479. Bouba Diop, No. 480. Taylor, No. 481. Kranjcar, No. 482. Mendes, No. 483. Davis, No. 484. Muntari, No. 485. Mwaruwari, No. 486. Nugent, No. 487. Utaka, No. 488. Kanu.

MERLIN. 2007/08.
Merlin's Kick Off 2007/08 Sticker Collection

230 stickers. No. 165. David James, No. 166. Sol Campbell, No. 167. Dejan Stefanovic, No. 168. Sylvain Distin, No. 169. Niko Kranjcar, No. 170. Matthew Taylor, No. 171. Sulley Muntari, No. 172. Gary O'Neil, No. 173. John Utaka,

No. 174. David Nugent, No. 175. Benjani Mwaruwari.

TOPPS. 2007/08.
Match Attax Trading Card Game

562 cards. Unnumbered. *Base Set:* David James, Glen Johnson, Hermann Hreidarsson, Lauren, Martin Cranie, Sylvain Distin, Noe Pamarot, Djimi Traore, Niko Kranjcar, Pedro Mendes, Sean Davis, Sulley Muntari, Benjamin Mwaruwari, David Nugent, John Utaka, Kanu. *New Signings:* Lassana Diarra, Milan Baros, Jermain Defoe. *Squad Updates:* Papa Bouba Diop. *Club Captains:* Sol Campbell. *Star Players:* Sol Campbell, Matthew Taylor. *Man of the Match:* David James, Matthew Taylor, David Nugent. *Limited Edition:* Sulley Muntari.

TOPPS. 2008/09.
Match Attax Trading Card Game

447 cards. Unnumbered. *Base Set:* David James, Glen Johnson, Hermann Hreidarsson, Lauren, Sylvain Distin, Younes Kaboul, Glen Little, Lassana Diarra, Niko Kranjcar, Papa Bouba Diop, Arnold Mvuemba, Jerome Thomas, Sean Davis, Peter Crouch, Ben Sahar, John Utaka, Sol Campbell. *Star Players:* Jermain Defoe, Lassana Diarra. *Man of the Match:* Niko Kranjcar, Jermain Defoe. *Limited Edition:* Peter Crouch.

TOPPS. 2008/09.
Total Football 2009 Premier League Sticker Collection

480 stickers. No. 226. Home Kit & Away Kit, No. 246. Peter Crouch, No. 265. David James, No. 334. Badge, No. 335. Team, *Star Player:* No. 336. Jermain Defoe. No. 337. David James, No. 338. Sol Campbell, No. 339. Sylvain Distin, No. 340. Armand Traore, No. 341. Hermann Hreidarsson, No. 342. Glen Johnson, No. 343. Younes Kaboul, No. 344. Lassana Diarra, No. 345. Sean Davis, No. 346. Papa Bouba Diop, No. 347. Richard Hughes, No. 348. Niko Kranjcar, No. 349. Arnold Mvuemba, No. 350. Jerome Thomas, No. 351. John Utaka, No. 352. Peter Crouch, No. 353. Jermain Defoe, No. 354. Kanu. *Topps Authentic Autograph:* No. 342. Glen Johnson.

TOPPS. 2009/10.
Match Attax Trading Card Game

444 cards. Unnumbered. *Base Set:* David James, Steve Finnan, Hermann Hreidarsson, Marc Wilson, Nadir Belhadj, Younes Kaboul, Joel Ward, Aaron Mokoena, Hayden Mullins, Angelos Basinas, Michael Brown, Richard Hughes, Frederic Piquionne, Aruna Dindane, John Utaka, Kanu. *Squad Updates:* Anthony Vanden Borre, Tal Ben Haim, Hassan Yebda, Jamie O'Hara, Kevin-Prince Boateng, Danny Webber. *Man of the Match:* Aaron Mokoena, Aruna Dindane, Nadir Belhadj, Younes Kaboul, Michael Brown. *Club Captains:* Aaron Mokoena. *i-Cards:* Tommy Smith, Papa Bouba Diop, Frederic Piquionne. *Manager:* Paul Hart. *Manager Update:* Avram Grant.

TOPPS. 2009/10.
Premier League Official 2010 Sticker Collection

462 stickers. No. 226. Kit, No. 246. Fratton Park, No. 316. Badge, No. 317. Team, *Star Player:* No. 318. David James. No. 319. David James, No. 320. Steve Finnan, No. 321. Hermann Hreidarsson, No. 322. Nadir Belhadj, No. 323. Younes Kaboul, No. 324. Tal Ben Haim, No. 325. Marc Wilson, No. 326. Jamie O'Hara, No. 327. Papa Bouba Diop, No. 328. Hassan Yebda, No. 329. Michael Brown, No. 330. Aaron Mokoena, No. 331. Tommy Smith, No. 332. Frederic Piquionne, No. 333. Kevin-Prince Boateng, No. 334. Aruna Dindane, No. 335. Danny Webber, No. 336. Kanu.

PANINI. 2010/11.
nPower Championship Official Sticker Collection 2011

386 stickers. No. 259. Badge, No. 260. Kits, No. 261. Team, No. 262A. Jamie Ashdown, No. 262B. Carl Dickinson, No. 263A. Aaron Mokoena, No. 263B. Hermann Hreidarsson, No. 264A. Joel Ward, No. 264B. Ibrahima Sonko, No. 265A. Ricardo Rocha, No. 265B. Liam Lawrence, No. 266A. Hayden Mullins, No. 266B. Michael Brown, No. 267A. Richard Hughes, No. 267B. Danny Webber, *Star Players:* No. 268. Dave Kitson, No. 269. Michael Brown. No. 270A. David Nugent, No. 270B. John Utaka, No. 271A. Dave Kitson, No. 271B. Kanu, *Club Captain:* No. 272/273. Aaron Mokoena. *International:* No. 289. Liam Lawrence.

TOPPS. 2011/12.
Match Attax Trading Card Game Championship Edition

293 cards. Unnumbered. Jamie Ashdown, Aaron Mokoena, Greg Halford, Hayden Mullins, Liam Lawrence, David Norris, Benjani, Dave Kitson, *Manager:* Michael Appleton, *Man of the Match:* Liam Lawrence, *Star Player:* Tal Ben Haim, Luke Varney.

TOPPS/PORTSMOUTH FC. 2017.
Portsmouth FC 2016/17 Trading Cards

27 Cards. Unnumbered. Badge, Fratton Park, Paul Cook, David Forde, Tom Davies, Enda Stevens, Danny Rose, Matt Clarke, Christian Burgess, Carl Baker, Michael Doyle, Gary Roberts, Liam O'Brien, Curtis Main, Nicke Kabamba, Jack Whatmough, Eoin Doyle, Jamal Lowe, Conor Chaplin, Noel Hunt, Kal Naismith, Kyle Bennett, Amine Linganzi, Drew Talbot, Gareth Evans, Stanley Aborah, Brandon Haunstrup.

TOPPS/PORTSMOUTH FC. 2019.
Portsmouth FC 2019 Collector Cards

30 Cards. No. 1. Badge, No. 2. Fratton Park, No. 3. Kenny Jackett, No. 4. Joe Gallen, No. 5. Luke McGee, No. 6. Craig MacGillivray, No. 7. Alex Bass, No. 8. Anton Walkes, No. 9. Lee Brown, No. 10. Matt Clarke, No. 11. Christian Burgess, No. 12. Jack Whatmough, No. 13. Nathan Thompson, No. 14. Brandon Haunstrup, No. 15. Tom Naylor, No. 16. Jamal Lowe, No. 17. Ronan Curtis, No. 18. Andy Cannon, No. 19. Dion Donohue, No. 20. Louis Dennis, No. 21. Viv Solomon-Otabor, No. 22. Bryn Morris, No. 23. Gareth Evans, No. 24. Adam May, No. 25. Ben Close, No. 26. Lloyd Isgrove, No. 27. Omar Bogle, No. 28. Brett Pitman, No. 29. Oli Hawkins, No. 30. James Vaughan.

TOPPS/PORTSMOUTH FC. 2019.
Portsmouth FC Checkatrade Trophy Winners 2019. Shirt Cards and Shirt/ Autograph Cards

14 cards (signed and unsigned). #/180. No. 1. Craig MacGillivray, No. 2. Lee Brown, No. 3. Matt Clarke, No. 4. Christian Burgess, No. 5. Nathan Thompson, No. 6. Tom Naylor, No. 7. Jamal Lowe, No. 8. Ronan Curtis, No. 9. Ben Close, No. 10. Omar Bogle, No. 11. Brett Pitman, No. 12. Anton Walkes, No. 13. Gareth Evans, No. 14. Oli Hawkins.

TOPPS/PORTSMOUTH FC. 2020.
Portsmouth FC 2019/20 Collector Cards

29 cards (signed and unsigned). Unnumbered. Alex Bass, Andy Cannon, Anton Walkes, Ben Close, Brandon Haunstrup, Brett Pitman, Tom Naylor, Christian Burgess, Craig MacGillivray, Ellis Harrison, Gareth Evans, James Bolton, John Marquis, Sean Raggett, Lee Brown, Marcus Harness, Oliver Hawkins, Paul Downing, Ronan Curtis, Ross McCrorie, Ryan Williams, Jack Whatmough, Bryn Morris, Luke McGee, Matt Casey, Kenny Jackett, Joe Gallen, Badge, Fratton Park. *New Signings Booster Pack:* Cameron McGeehan, Reeco Hackett-Fairchild, Steve Seddon.

TOPPS/PORTSMOUTH FC. 2021.
Portsmouth FC 2020/21 Collector Cards

28 cards (signed and unsigned). Unnumbered. Michael Jacobs, Alex Bass, Andy Cannon, Ben Close, Bryn Morris, John Marquis, Callum Johnson, Duncan Turnbull, Craig MacGillivray, Haji Mnoga, Jack Whatmough, James Bolton, Jordy Hiwula, Marcus Harness, Paul Downing, Rasmus Nicolaisen, Ronan Curtis, Sean Raggett, Tom Naylor, Ellis Harrison, Harvey White, Lee Brown, Ryan Williams, George Byers, Charlie Daniels, Lewis Ward, Kenny Jackett, Joe Gallen. *Booster Pack:* Danny Cowley, Nicky Cowley.

TOPPS/PORTSMOUTH FC. 2021/22.
2021/22 Portsmouth FC – Topps Now

19 base cards. No. 001. Connor Ogilvie – 11.12.2021 – print run: 73, No. 002. Gavin Bazunu – 03.01.2022 – print run: 406, No. 003. Ronan Curtis – 07.01.2022 – print run: 92, No. 004. Hayden Carter/Tyler Walker – 18.01.2022 – print run: 54, No. 005. Denver Hume – 31.01.2022 – print run: 49, No. 006. Michael Jacobs – 08.02.2022 – print run: 56, No. 007. Aiden O'Brien – 26.02.2022 – print run: 60, No. 008. Hayden Carter – 01.03.2022 – print run: 57, No. 009. Sean Raggett – 05.03.2022 – print run: 11, No. 010. George Hirst – 05.03.2022 – print run: 31, No. 011. Jay Mingi – 05.03.2022 – print run: 106. *Parallel cards:* black #/99, blue #/10, gold 1/1. No. 012. Tyler Walker – 08.03.2022 – print run: 41, No. 013. George Hirst – 08.03.2022 – print run: 40, No. 014. Clark Robertson – 12.04.2022 – print run: 51, No. 015. Portsmouth FC – 12.04.2022 – print run: 45, No. 016. Ronan Curtis – 15.04.2022 – print run: 49, No. 017. Ronan Curtis – 23.04.2022 – print run: 100. *Parallel card:* blue #/50, No. 018. George Hurst – 26.04.2022 – print run: 47, No. 019. Aiden O'Brien – 26.04.2022 – print run: 48.